A GENESIS TO REVELATION

GUIDE
TO Prayer

PAMELA L. MCQUADE

BARBOUR BOOKS
An Imprint of Barbour Publishing, Inc.

Published by Barbour Books, an imprint of Barbour Publishing, Inc., 1810 Barbour Drive, Uhrichsville, Ohio 44683, www.barbourbooks.com

Our mission is to inspire the world with the life-changing message of the Bible.

Member of the
Evangelical Christian
Publishers Association

Contents

INTRODUCTION:

CONVERSATIONS WITH GOD

Prayer can perhaps be the greatest joy of the Christian life, because communicating with God in an intimate way far outdoes any conversation we could have with people. And as we consistently talk to God, we draw closer to Him every day. Prayer is our lifeline.

Why, then, can it be such a struggle to set aside time for communion with our Lord? Why do we find it so hard to run to Him every day? Wouldn't you think that prayer should be joyous and easy? But for many of us, more often than we'd like to admit, it isn't.

True, there are times when we enjoy prayer, and our communication with God runs smoothly. Those days encourage us to want to commune with Him regularly. But we do not have to be long in the faith before we experience some common challenges to our prayer lives.

During those dry periods, we might look at prayer as a spiritual version of a muscle builder. Many of us struggle to make physical exercise a part of our days, and we can struggle to keep up our regular conversation with God too. But both are needful, even though the benefits of prayer far outweigh anything we do in the physical realm.

Has anyone ever declared that prayer was easy? Only an unwise person, someone who who has not experienced the complexities of our Lord and the perplexities of humanity, would make that frivolous claim. Because it's part of a relationship between our glorious Lord and His fallen people, prayer is as complex as God is. But despite our many weaknesses and failings, He has invited us into this connection with Himself. We neglect it at our own risk.

When we do pray, it seems natural to ask God for help. But our ongoing conversation with God should be more than asking Him for everything we want, as if we were greedy children. Praise, thanksgiving, confession, and the placing of spiritual and physical needs—ours, and the needs of others—before God are all part of a balanced prayer conversation.

In the Old and New Testaments, we see many examples of prayer. Kings offered up praise to God, and the apostles gave thanks for His provision for the people's needs. More intimately, individuals asked God for help, thanked Him for His response, and praised His faithfulness. In his psalms, David shows us the faithfulness of God, and the Gospels demonstrate the importance of prayer in the life of Jesus. Taken as a whole, the Bible teaches us how to pray effectively.

Prayer is more than the words we think or speak—it's a relationship with our God. When we communicate with Him, either aloud or in our minds, we trust that He does exist and that He will answer prayer. But whether or not He gives what we ask, we trust that He is leading us on the best path—that even though we may face struggles today, He only has good things in mind for us.

Just as our human relationships can be challenging, so can our prayer relationship with God. We don't always understand Him. . .in fact, we *can't* entirely understand Him, since He's God! But we would never think of giving up on a child who doesn't understand life's challenges, and God will not give up on us either. If we wander away from prayer, He calls us back to relationship. As we respond, the roadblocks will eventually clear. In time, we may finally grasp why prayer had become so difficult and how faithful God had been to us.

Wherever you are in your Christian life, join me in seeking to know more about the joys and challenges of prayer. Let's rejoice together in the Lord who seeks to commune with us.

1. Pray Without Ceasing

Though we may feel intimidated about praying to an almighty, all-knowing God, His Word tells us to "pray without ceasing" (1 Thessalonians 5:17). In just one example of that, the Bible describes the early church praying for Peter, their leader, who'd been jailed for sharing the faith: "Peter therefore was kept in prison: but prayer was made without ceasing of the church unto God for him" (Acts 12:5).

Here's some good news: no one in our lives has to be jailed for us to start praying. God wants to hear from us anytime, whether it's a five-star day or a major bummer. He desires an intimate relationship with us and invites us to draw near. We can have a sense of excitement about our communication with God, because He delights in knowing us. God *wants* us to talk to Him.

"Oh, but I can't share everything with God," you may worry as you think of a particularly knotty problem. If so, remind yourself constantly of this verse: "Cast all your anxiety on him because he cares for you" (1 Peter 5:7 NIV). The Lord who loves you and called you to Himself invites you to share every trial and temptation with Him. Worry is unnecessary. God takes pleasure in responding to the needs of His beloved.

For Christians, nothing need separate us from God's help and support. Once we have prayed the first true prayer, inviting Him into our hearts, God calls us to deep, ongoing communion with Him: "Trust in Him at all times, you people; pour out your heart before Him; God is a refuge for us" (Psalm 62:8 NKJV). Quite simply, if we pray in faith, we can expect answers: "And all things, whatsoever ye shall ask in prayer, believing, ye shall receive" (Matthew 21:22).

THE ELEMENTS OF PRAYER

But what is prayer, and how should we pray?

Prayer is not simply asking God for good things and expecting Him to respond. That's an aspect of prayer, but it must also include an appreciation for God and His greatness that leads us into praise for who He is and what He has done. We praise the One who has done so much for His children—all those who have trusted in the sacrifice of His Son, Jesus, for their salvation. We delight in the power, mercy, and love of a God who didn't need to reach down to sinful people but still made us His dearly loved children.

As we communicate with God, we recognize more and more of His holiness and goodness—and more and more of our own failures. Then we seek His forgiveness so we can walk away from our prayer place with a new, clean heart. Any time we do wrong, we can wipe the slate and start anew with God, based on His forgiveness. Only a clean heart is ready to come to God with every need.

Next, as we see God's work in our lives, we give thanks. No relationship runs smoothly without appreciation for what another has done, and this is true with God as well. We have much to be thankful for: "O give thanks unto the LORD; for he is good: for his mercy endureth for ever" (Psalm 136:1).

Thanksgiving is not just an extra element of prayer, something that can be ignored when we choose. The apostle Paul reminded Christians in Thessalonica not to fail in their gratitude: "In every thing give thanks: for this is the will of God in Christ Jesus concerning you" (1 Thessalonians 5:18). No matter what is happening in our lives, we can always find something to thank God for. In fact, sometimes the darker moments make us more aware of how much God has done throughout our lives and how grateful we are for His presence.

Finally, in prayer we bring our needs before God, asking Him to provide for us and help us in our spiritual and physical needs.

These elements of prayer have been described with the acronym ACTS:

- Adoration (I have called this Praise)
- Confession
- Thanksgiving
- Supplication

This four-part guide is a good reminder of what elements should be part of our praying. But prayers do not always fall neatly into these categories, and often we will jump from one point to another. For example, as we confess our sins, praise may spring up in our minds, and we'll return to adoration for a while. Or when needs trouble our spirit, we may bring them to the Lord before we give thanks for the good things He's already done in our lives.

Still, the acrostic is a useful tool to make sure we do not get caught up in selfish requests, forgetting to praise the Lord who has given us so much. Balanced prayer helps us consider the work of God in our lives and the world, encouraging us to seek the good of others in our requests. Our communion with God becomes a ministry that influences others' lives.

PRAYER AND COMMUNITY

Prayer is a key part of the larger picture of faith—community. Though it is not the only thing we need to do to be effective in the Christian life, communion with God helps us pull together many elements that Paul mentions in Romans 12:9–13 (NKJV):

> *Let love be without hypocrisy. Abhor what is evil. Cling to what is good. Be kindly affectionate to one another with brotherly love, in honor giving preference to one another; not lagging in diligence, fervent in spirit, serving the Lord; rejoicing in hope, patient in tribulation, continuing steadfastly in prayer; distributing to the needs of the saints, given to hospitality.*

As we pray, our hearts become warm toward God and other people. Evil begins to horrify us, and we turn toward good. As a result, we treat others well and serve God fervently in the many ways this passage describes. Prayer is not just words on our lips or in our hearts—it's also part of our actions as a result of our communion with divinity.

Life often becomes difficult. But when we communicate freely with God, we find strength and wisdom to deal with the hardships. Though our experience with family, friends, and fellow believers may be less than perfect, God's Spirit can ease those relationships in a way we would never have imagined before we knew Christ. And as we treat others with Christian love, they'll have a hard time not appreciating the kindness, mercy, and caring that God has put in our hearts.

Prayer is not some airy-fairy element of faith— it provides sustenance for the down-to-earth service we give to God every day. When we regularly spend time with Him, we begin to see His work in our lives and our world. We'll recognize His answers to the specific prayers we've prayed.

But a few prayer victories must never lead to laxness. "Pray without ceasing" should be the watchword of our lives. It is a privilege granted only to those who have asked God to be part of their lives and are willing to connect with Him often.

2. BENEFITS OF PRAYER

"How am I supposed to pray ceaselessly?" you may be wondering. "Life is already so busy it's hard to find time to communicate with my family, much less God."

Despite our doubts, scripture tells us to pray at all times. Why? Because not praying means we'll develop only a flaccid Christian life. When we don't take prayer seriously, we aren't taking God seriously. Our spiritual lives will suffer for that.

GOD-CENTERED PRAYER

When our prayer life slacks off, we often find ourselves unhappy with our faith. After all, our lives are designed to be centered on Christ, so when we fail to communicate with Him, we have a distant, rather empty relationship with our Lord.

However, as we open our lives to God through prayer, we deepen our rapport and friendship. Bringing our needs before Him and thanking, praising, and worshipping Him all give us a proper view of our relationship to the Lord. He is the mighty God, and we are His creation—yet He has invited us to ask Him into our lives and to be part of His. A sense of humility allows us to know God more deeply.

When we communicate with Him, our Lord can work on our attitudes. But if we shut Him out, we are unlikely to grow much in our faith or become the people, spiritually speaking, that we should be. To put it in the simplest terms, we benefit from prayer more than God does.

PRAYER AND OUR OTHER RELATIONSHIPS

Our communion with God improves more than just our relationship with Him. It also benefits our relationship with others as the fruit of God's Spirit develops in our day-to-day lives. When we live for Him, our relationships with other people—even those who disagree with us—often take on a gentler, more appealing aspect.

In prayer, as we see our own failings and shortcomings, God quietly but firmly sends us in the direction we need to go. Whether in interpersonal relationships, our work lives, or our spiritual journeys, we begin to live in a more godly fashion. And we are blessed by that lifestyle change.

Helping others by praying for them—and then seeing God act in their lives—improves our own lives. When we feel down, it's wonderful to see how effectively God is working in another person's life, and we can take hope from that. When our spirits are high, we can enjoy the testimony of God's work in a fellow Christian's life and then share that truth with others.

THE PERSONAL BLESSING OF PRAYER

God blesses us as we pray regularly and fervently. If we seek His face, He responds, and we go places spiritually that we might never have imagined. As we see God's responses to our prayers, we are encouraged by the closeness of our relationship and the many blessings He's bestowed on us. That motivates us to pray even more. We'll find time for prayer, though our lives remain busy.

Perhaps the greatest benefit of our communion with God is the joy it brings into our lives. As we thank God for our salvation and the way He's worked in our lives, our delight is a form of praise. Praise should be a part of our daily Christian experience. When we live this way, others will see God's glory, even if we never say a word.

Some days, we may have to make a great effort to meet with God, or we might not spend a long time communing when we do. But regular, committed prayer will be worth the effort we put into it. If we can pray when life becomes tense and challenging, surely we can make time even in happier circumstances.

The many benefits of prayer—in our own lives, and in the world around us—should motivate us to talk with God regularly. But if you need even more encouragement to pray, let's look now at prayer throughout the Bible.

3. An Overview of Prayer in the Bible

Prayer appears throughout the Bible, so let's take a Genesis-to-Revelation tour to see what each book shows about communication with God.

Each biblical writer had his own take on prayer. Some offered a lot of advice about how to pray and what to say to God; others just hinted at prayer in difficult situations. But behind the scenes, even in those books where prayer is barely mentioned, we can see the effects of knowing God and spending time with Him.

GENESIS

Early in human history, sometime after the birth of Adam's grandson Enos, prayer and worship became part of the lives of God's people: "then began men to call upon the name of the Lord" (Genesis 4:26). In Genesis we see some early steps in people's communication with their Creator. When God instituted His covenant with Abram, He began with a promise that He would bless those who followed Him. So we see that prayer and obedience are closely connected.

Exodus

In Exodus, prayer follows the ups and downs of the lives of the Hebrew people, the descendants of Abraham. When they were in subjection to Egypt's harsh ruler, they groaned for God's help. Delivered from Egypt, their voices rose in praise. The prophet Moses is the most powerful prayer, faithfully intervening for his people when they fell away from God.

Leviticus

Leviticus is a book of laws telling priests how sacrifices should be made and what the people should do to follow God. Since the book focuses on rules for holiness, specific prayers do not appear—but it is hard to imagine a proper focus on God could occur without the priests having regular communication with Him.

Numbers

Though prayer is not a large part of the book of Numbers, we see some powerful praying by the prophet Moses, usually when he asked God to save His people. But we also find the example of Balaam, who prayed, got direction from God, and still ended up disobeying Him.

DEUTERONOMY

In this book, through the example of Moses, God taught His people about prayer by showing the Hebrews how praise should look.

JOSHUA

In Joshua, most of the praying was done by Moses' successor as he sought to lead the Israelites into faithfulness. In chapter 7, as Joshua prayed for a disobedient people, he repeated Moses' argument that God should not destroy His unfaithful ones, since pagan nations would perceive that as faithlessness on God's part. (God solved the problem by separating out the sinners who caused Israel to lose a battle and punishing them alone.) In Joshua 10:12–13, Israel's leader prayed that the sun would stay in the sky until a battle ended, and God did so, holding the sun in place for a whole day.

JUDGES

The book of Judges shows the vacillating habits of God's people, who would go to Him in prayer when times were difficult and stray away when life seemed good. Although the prophets encouraged the Hebrews to remain faithful, they were easily distracted unless life became hard. So, often, God did not give them an easy road.

RUTH

The book of Ruth does not record any prayers, but it is filled with incidents that seem like answers to prayer. Consider these events: widowed Ruth stays with her widowed mother-in-law, Naomi, though she'd been urged to leave; wealthy Boaz protects and marries Ruth; Naomi enjoys a grandson through her daughter-in-law's marriage to Boaz. Each seems like something poor, desperate women would have asked God for.

1 SAMUEL

This book begins with the story of a woman praying desperately for a child. Her prayers were so raw that she was accused of being drunk! But Hannah persisted, and God gave her the son she requested. The boy, Samuel, responded to God's call, went on to lead Israel, and interceded for the Hebrews when they failed God. Finally, he encouraged the people not to turn from God but to be faithful in prayer. Though Samuel tried to lead King Saul in the right path, things went terribly wrong and God ultimately revealed a new king, David. David had a strong prayer relationship with God as evidenced by the psalms he wrote.

2 SAMUEL

As the anointed but yet-to-be crowned king of Israel, David faced many battles and challenges through intense prayer. Unlike Saul, King David's decision-making was bathed in communication with God. And even when David sinned, he eventually turned to God in confession.

1 KINGS

This historical book contains powerful examples of prayer by a king and a prophet. Solomon, offered the opportunity to ask God for anything, prayed for the wisdom to rule well. Afterward, he led his people in praise at the consecration of the temple. Through prayer the prophet Elijah raised a dead boy back to life and defeated the prophets of the false god Baal.

2 KINGS

Prayers in this book, though not frequent, are powerful. Elisha prayed for the life of the Shunnamite woman's son, and God restored him. Elisha, in the city of Dothan, also prayed for his servant to see God's protection, and the Lord showed him horses and chariots of fire that surrounded the city. When he was very ill, King Hezekiah prayed that God would extend his life, and the Lord did so.

1 CHRONICLES

As with the Bible's other history books, this one gives powerful examples of prayers in Israel's history. Jabez prayed for blessing, and God freely answered him. David humbly thanked God for the promise that his son Solomon would build the magnificent temple in Jerusalem; then he prayed before the people about the planned project and about God's greatness.

2 CHRONICLES

In 2 Chronicles we see the prayers of kings. Attacked by the Ethiopians, Judah's King Asa prayed for God's help and saw Him save the nation. Publicly, King Jehoshaphat encouraged his people to cry out to God in their need. And when idolatrous King Manasseh recognized his error, 2 Chronicles 33:13 reports his prayer of repentance.

EZRA

Most of Ezra's prayers are of repentance. The book starts with the Jews, who had been conquered by the Babylonians and taken away as prisoners, establishing a right attitude toward God as they set off for their homeland. Ezra proclaimed a fast, urging the people to humble themselves and pray for God's protection. Back in Judah, Ezra publicly expressed a prayer of repentance for the people who had remained in the land and sinned by intermarrying with pagans. The wrongdoers repented and put aside their unbelieving wives.

Nehemiah

As cupbearer to Persian king Artaxerxes, Nehemiah heard of the trouble the people who'd remained in Judah were facing, and he wept, mourned, fasted, and prayed. Confessing the sins of his fellow Jews, he asked God to send him and the other exiles back to their own nation. When Artaxerxes asked why Nehemiah seemed upset, the cupbearer sent up a quick prayer for God's help and explained the situation to the king. God answered Nehemiah's prayer, softening the ruler's heart to allow Nehemiah and others to return to Jerusalem to rebuild the temple. As the work began, men of other nations objected—so the people of Judah, fearing an attack, prayed as they worked. God answered the prayer by giving the workers remarkable success.

Esther

Though neither prayer nor God are specifically mentioned in Esther, both are obviously behind the scenes. The faithful queen likely prayed quietly and privately, as her actions show strong faith in

God. When she called her women to fast while she prepared to visit the king, they probably also prayed, as Esther herself surely did.

JOB

Job had many reasons to pray as he faced the loss of almost everything of value to him. But he never lost faith in God, and ultimately heard God Himself answers his cries. In the end, Job had many reasons to rejoice—not the least of them the deepening of his relationship with God.

PSALMS

Psalms is the songbook of the Bible, and much of it focuses on prayer and praise for God's goodness and power. There is inspiration for prayer in all the psalms. When we struggle with prayer, it is an excellent book to read—it's hard not to find praise welling up in your mind and heart when you read this book.

PROVERBS

Though there are no specific prayers in Proverbs, there is plenty of wisdom about how we should please God, ideas that will help us know how to pray in God's will. If Proverbs describes a lifestyle that God tells us to make part of our lives, prayer can help us to live that way.

ECCLESIASTES

Ecclesiastes shows believers how empty the world is apart from the Lord and how necessary God is in their lives. Though there is no direct reference to prayer, it is clear that relationship with and obedience to God is important. Communication with God would naturally be part of that picture.

SONG OF SOLOMON

Though the lovers in the Song of Solomon do not speak prayers to God, this book has been seen as a picture of the love relationship between God and His people. Closeness in our relationship with God depends on communion with our Lord.

ISAIAH

In a disastrous time for Judah, God provided the prophet Isaiah, through whom He offered both correction and encouragement. Isaiah's communication with God shows the intimate relationship he had with his Lord and encourages all who face times of trouble.

JEREMIAH

Jeremiah prophesied to God's people both before and after many of the Jews were transported to Babylon; his book portrays the relationship between himself and God. Though God had the larger part of the conversation, Jeremiah was not afraid to express the needs and fears of his countrymen, even after God told him not to pray for these unregenerate people. The prophet understood why God was angry with His people, but he also understood the people's doubts and fears. When Jeremiah was attacked by some of his own, he went to God in his pain and prayed for their salvation.

LAMENTATIONS

In his lamentations, Jeremiah poured out his own sin and torment to God and asked for forgiveness. Later the prophet encouraged his people—the nation of Judah—to do the same, despite the awful things their conquerors had done.

EZEKIEL

God communicated with this man, a prophet among the exiled Jews in Babylon, in a series of visions that must have stunned Ezekiel. More often than not, he simply listened to God rather than praying, and then he recorded God's message. But when the prophet did engage in prayer, he begged mercy for God's fallen and distant people.

DANIEL

Daniel was a man who knew the power of prayer, engaging in prayer even though it made life dangerous. When the Babylonian king, Nebuchadnezzar, wanted to kill all his wise men because they couldn't describe his troubling dream, Daniel stepped up, first asking his Jewish friends to pray for him. When the Median king, Darius, foolishly made prayer to anyone but him illegal, Daniel still opened his windows and prayed publicly to the Lord. That decision landed him in the lions' den.

HOSEA

Prayer is not a large topic in the book of Hosea. Most of the book discusses God's judgment of His faithless people and pronouncements against them, contrasted with ever-present love and forgiveness. Life without prayer is empty as demonstrated in the lives of God's faithless people.

JOEL

Joel is an example of prayer: in the first chapter of his book, he cries out to God when destruction rains down on the land. In Joel 2:17, the prophet calls on the priests to pray for their land. As a result of their prayers, God relented and promised that great blessings would follow Judah's repentance.

Amos

The people of the northern Jewish kingdom of Israel, to whom Amos preached, were not big on praying to God, though they spent plenty of time before pagan idols. The prophet's repeated efforts to turn them to repentance went unheeded, and eventually all he could do was pray that God would forgive His people and not destroy the land.

Obadiah

In this prophecy against the Edomites, who were related to but enemies of the Israelites, God promised to defend His people. Since the brief message is directed to enemies of God, there is no praying in evidence.

Jonah

The book of Jonah relates prayers of repentance, both by Jonah and the powerful but wicked people of Nineveh. God is willing to forgive even His enemies, if they admit their guilt to Him.

Micah

Micah describes a people so lost in sin that they do not even seem to recognize it. The book is a picture of a mostly prayerless people who cannot get an answer from God.

Nahum

This book describes the downfall of Nineveh at God's hands. The people of Assyria do not believe in the Lord and do not pray to Him.

Habakkuk

Habakkuk is a book of prayer. First, the prophet confronts God about the violence in society while He seems to do nothing. In the end, the prophet praises the strength of God.

Zephaniah

In this prophecy about the destruction of nations by the Assyrians, there is only a promised day of worship, when those who worship God will bring offerings and no doubt pray. In that day, humble Jerusalem will rejoice (3:14).

Haggai

Haggai encouraged the Jews who returned to Jerusalem to rebuild the temple. God was determined to have a place where He would be worshipped. No doubt the building of the temple encouraged the people to think of Him and begin their worship, including prayer.

ZECHARIAH

Zechariah, Haggai's contemporary, called the people back to God. Though he painted God's blessings to come in broad brushstrokes, the discouraged people were hard to motivate. Prayer was only an underlying theme, to be found in the promises of worship.

MALACHI

God repeated His promises to bless His discouraged people, who returned to a destroyed land. But He also made clear that He would not tolerate actions that did not reflect His truth and character. The people are described as talking with God, but in arrogance and self-justification rather than in true prayer.

MATTHEW

The book of Matthew is filled with prayer; for example, it is one of two Gospels to record the Lord's Prayer. People who met Jesus face-to-face had an unusual opportunity to ask Him personally for whatever they needed, and He answered. But God is no less interested in listening to our needs today.

Mark

In Mark, as we see how Jesus prays, we gain our ultimate example in prayer. Jesus is also shown responding to the needs of many who called on Him for help.

Luke

Luke provides numerous examples of people glorifying God and coming to Jesus with requests, which might be considered prayer. Here too we have the Lord's Prayer (also described in Matthew), the parable of the prayers of a Pharisee and a tax collector, and Jesus' request for forgiveness for those who put Him on the cross.

John

From John we receive an understanding of the power of prayer in the life of the believer. Jesus is shown praying for God's will in the Garden of Gethsemane, just ahead of the Lord's own sacrifice on the cross. Jesus also prayed for His disciples as they would soon face a time without Him.

Acts

The first-century church was a praying body, for prayer was their lifeline to God in a world of persecution. Here we see the best foundation for a church as the apostles gave themselves continually to prayer (Acts 6:4).

ROMANS

Though Paul had not been to Rome when he wrote this letter, he could still have a deep relationship with these people through prayer. The apostle gave the Romans directions on how to pray and encouraged them to be faithful in prayer. He also humbly asked the fledgling church to pray for his needs in his stressful ministry.

1 CORINTHIANS

The Corinthian congregation might be called Paul's "bad-boy church." This book of the Bible had to deal with thorny issues, such as whether women should pray with heads covered or uncovered. While that's not a big issue in today's church, Paul shared other wisdom on prayer and speaking in tongues, which people do still debate.

2 CORINTHIANS

Though Paul had his differences with the Corinthian church, he also recognized their place in God's work and depended on them to support him with prayer. No doubt the apostle recognized that no church is perfect, but God can still work through each one.

GALATIANS

The book of Galatians deals with a doctrinal mess caused by the "Judaizers," who had visited the Galatian church to urge believers to obey all the Jewish traditions and law in addition to the gospel. Paul doubtless prayed for the church, though the only recorded prayer is a concluding blessing.

EPHESIANS

In Ephesians the apostle Paul encouraged believers to know God deeply both by understanding what He has done for them and expressing appreciation through prayer and worship. "I pray that the eyes of your heart may be enlightened," he wrote, "in order that you may know the hope to which he has called you, the riches of his glorious inheritance in his holy people, and his incomparably great power for us who believe" (1:18–19 NIV).

PHILIPPIANS

Paul gave thanks for the faith of the Philippians and encouraged them in prayer. As they prayed, Paul promised that God would meet their needs according to His riches, not the believers' natural abilities.

COLOSSIANS

During his first imprisonment in Rome, Paul wrote to the Colossians to correct some heresy the church had fallen into. He began with a prayerful benediction that reminded his readers what they should believe, and he told them that he had always prayed for them. In the last chapter, Paul called for prayer both for their own spiritual neediness and his ministry.

1 THESSALONIANS

All the prayers in Paul's first letter to the Thessalonians are for the people of this church. From his example they learned what it means to pray fervently and thankfully.

2 THESSALONIANS

Though the bulk of the praying in this letter is for the church in Thessalonica, Paul also asked for prayer that would support his ministry and see it grow.

1 TIMOTHY

This book has only two mentions of prayer, but from them we learn the importance of praying for leaders and the ability of prayer to consecrate our lives to God.

2 TIMOTHY

Paul told Timothy that he regularly prayed for his ministry, and shared with him some of the challenges he'd faced.

TITUS

This book of instruction and encouragement to a young man who was new in ministry does not focus on prayer, but as in all his letters, Paul gives a blessing for Titus.

PHILEMON

In this letter, Paul had a difficult task: he asked a slaveowner to have mercy on a runaway slave. Tactfully, the apostle told Philemon that he was always in his prayers—perhaps creating a bridge between the two men, who were likely to disagree on Paul's subject.

HEBREWS

References to prayer and worship in the book of Hebrews focus on the work of Christ and the Christian's everyday life.

JAMES

James encourages prayer in times of trouble, happiness, sickness, and sin, making the well-known statement, "The effectual fervent prayer of a righteous man availeth much" (5:16).

1 PETER

It may seem strange that the book of 1 Peter, written when Christians suffered intense persecution, does not focus on people's needs but rather the praise they should offer. Emphasizing our troubles will never help the way an appreciation for God will. Peter reminded his readers of the hope they have in the resurrection and the perfection that suffering in Christ brings to them.

2 PETER

In the first verses of this book, Peter requested that the grace and peace of God be given to his readers. This would enable them to "escape the corruption that is in the world" (1:4).

1 JOHN

In 1 John, prayer is implied rather than stated. But confession, praise, and worship are themes throughout the book. It would be a good book to pray through, since it includes so many truths that are helpful in the Christian life.

2 JOHN

This letter to the "elect lady" does not focus on prayer, but John hoped that God's blessing would be on her as she faced false teaching. Since these errors were common in the early church, doubtless John was praying for her and her church as they faced this situation.

3 JOHN

Gaius, the recipient of this letter of commendation and encouragement, had prospered spiritually, and John also commended him to God for his physical needs.

JUDE

Writing to Christians who found their faith assailed by false teachers, Jude reminded his readers of false teachers of the past and the prophecies of those who were to come. He encouraged them to respond in prayer inspired by the Holy Spirit, and he ended his epistle with praise to God.

REVELATION

Revelation includes many praises for the wonderful things God has done to save His people. Despite the dire prophecies in the book, God's people should be aware of the ultimate goal He has in mind and praise Him for our salvation through the death and resurrection of Jesus.

4. 144 References to Prayer

The Bible includes many references to prayer, including praise and worship as well as asking God for help or mercy. The following 144 passages give us a picture of what prayer and worship can be, and help us understand how we can pray effectively. We present the passages both in the King James Version language, as well as a more modern translation.

THE FIRST PRAYER

Why prayer, or calling on the name of the Lord, begins at the time of the birth of Adam's grandson Enos, the Bible doesn't say. But at this point, people sought to draw near to God. As subsequent chapters of Genesis show, God responded.

And to Seth, to him also there was born a son; and he called his name Enos: then began men to call upon the name of the LORD.
                                    GENESIS 4:26

Seth also had a son, and he named him Enosh. At that time people began to call on the name of the LORD.
                              GENESIS 4:26 NIV

WORSHIP AT AN ALTAR

After God showed Abram the land he would inhabit, Abram was overwhelmed with the Lord's grace. Once God commanded him to walk the land and look at it, Abram was moved to worship this generous God who had a plan for His people, so he set up an altar where God could receive praise.

Then Abram removed his tent, and came and dwelt in the plain of Mamre, which is in Hebron, and built there an altar unto the LORD.

GENESIS 13:18

So Abram moved his camp to Hebron and settled near the oak grove belonging to Mamre. There he built another altar to the LORD.

GENESIS 13:18 NLT

QUESTIONING GOD IN PRAYER

God had promised Abram an heir and a land, but this elderly and faithful man had yet to see either—so he questioned God about both promises. Yet as he questioned, Genesis 15:6 tells us that Abram also believed. Balancing his questions about life and God with faith in God made all the difference. The Lord gave Abram the promised heir and land, and He made both into a great nation.

> *And Abram said, Behold, to me thou hast given no seed: and, lo, one born in my house is mine heir. . . . And he said, LORD God, whereby shall I know that I shall inherit it?*
>
> GENESIS 15:3, 8

> *And Abram said, "You have given me no children; so a servant in my household will be my heir." . . . But Abram said, "Sovereign LORD, how can I know that I will gain possession of it?"*
>
> GENESIS 15:3, 8 NIV

PRAYER FOR SODOM

In one of the boldest prayers in scripture, Abraham asked God not to destroy the wicked city of Sodom. Abraham's nephew Lot lived there. Though Abraham started his prayer by asking God to spare the city if fifty good people lived there, he reduced the number several times until it reached just ten. Sadly, not even ten believers could be found, and God wiped Sodom away. Still, He saved Lot and some of his family, though even this kindness was eventually marred by the family's unbelief.

And Abraham drew near, and said,
Wilt thou also destroy the righteous with
the wicked? Peradventure there be fifty
righteous within the city: wilt thou also
destroy and not spare the place for the fifty
righteous that are therein?

GENESIS 18:23–24

And Abraham came near and said, "Would
You also destroy the righteous with the
wicked? Suppose there were fifty righteous
within the city; would You also destroy the
place and not spare it for the fifty righteous
that were in it?"

GENESIS 18:23–24 NKJV

One day, God called and Abraham answered. But this was a wrenching call: to sacrifice his miracle son, Isaac. Though it undoubtedly went against everything Abraham knew about God, the pained father did not disobey. He set out to make the sacrifice, trusting that even if God demanded his son, He could also raise Isaac from the dead. Abraham's willingness to respond to God with trust— to say, "Here I am"—brought a wonderful answer that did not require Isaac's life. In the moment he lifted the knife yet hoped in God, faithful Abraham became an example to all humanity. Even the son he loved dearly, the boy he'd waited so long to have, would not separate him from God.

> *And the angel of the LORD called unto him out of heaven, and said, Abraham, Abraham: and he said, Here am I. And he said, Lay not thine hand upon the lad, neither do thou any thing unto him: for now I know that thou fearest God, seeing thou hast not withheld thy son, thine only son from me.*
>
> GENESIS 22:11–12

> *But the angel of the LORD called out to him from heaven, "Abraham! Abraham!"*
> *"Here I am," he replied.*

*"Do not lay a hand on the boy," he said.
"Do not do anything to him. Now I know
that you fear God, because you have not
withheld from me your son, your only son."*

GENESIS 22:11–12 NIV

PRAYER AND RELATIONSHIP

Jacob knew he'd wronged his brother, Esau. When
God commanded Jacob to return to the land
where his brother lived, that became a big problem. Faced with Esau and his men, Jacob worried
about a confrontation. In his fear Jacob went to
God in prayer. Is it surprising that the meeting
between the brothers went more smoothly when
God was with them?

*Deliver me, I pray thee, from the hand of
my brother, from the hand of Esau: for I
fear him, lest he will come and smite me,
and the mother with the children.*

GENESIS 32:11

*"Save me, I pray, from the hand of my
brother Esau, for I am afraid he will come
and attack me, and also the mothers with
their children."*

GENESIS 32:11 NIV

Prayer in Deep Need

Israel's prayer time was not always sweet. In the nation's suffering during its bondage in Egypt, the people groaned to God, and He heard. God doesn't only answer prayers that are "properly" made—He responds to the needs of His people, even when they can barely groan. When His people most needed Him, the Bible shows us that God responded to the expression of their hearts.

> *And it came to pass in process of time, that the king of Egypt died: and the children of Israel sighed by reason of the bondage, and they cried, and their cry came up unto God by reason of the bondage. And God heard their groaning, and God remembered his covenant with Abraham, with Isaac, and with Jacob. And God looked upon the children of Israel, and God had respect unto them.*
>
> Exodus 2:23–25

> *Years passed, and the king of Egypt died. But the Israelites continued to groan under their burden of slavery. They cried out for help, and their cry rose up to God. God heard their groaning, and he remembered his covenant promise to Abraham, Isaac, and Jacob. He looked down on the people of Israel and knew it was time to act.*
>
> Exodus 2:23–25 NLT

PRAYER AS A RESPONSE TO GOD

When Moses turned aside from his shepherding to consider an amazing burning bush in the desert, God began a conversation with him. Moses proved he was open to the Lord, and he was commissioned to lead God's people out of Egypt and into the Promised Land.

> *And when the LORD saw that he turned aside to see, God called unto him out of the midst of the bush, and said, Moses, Moses. And he said, Here am I.*
>
> EXODUS 3:4

> *When the LORD saw that he had gone over to look, God called to him from within the bush, "Moses! Moses!" And Moses said, "Here I am."*
>
> EXODUS 3:4 NIV

PRAYER FOR DELIVERANCE

Though God had promised to deliver His people from Egypt, that didn't seem to be happening. If anything, the Hebrews had it much worse as the pharaoh piled work onto the already overburdened people. So Moses went to God in prayer to object. God certainly knew what was going on in Egypt, but He still expected Moses and the people to talk to Him about their troubles. In Exodus 6, God gave Moses a sneak peek at what He planned to do for His people.

And Moses returned unto the LORD, and said, LORD, wherefore hast thou so evil entreated this people? why is it that thou hast sent me? For since I came to Pharaoh to speak in thy name, he hath done evil to this people; neither hast thou delivered thy people at all.

EXODUS 5:22–23

Then Moses went back to the LORD and protested, "Why have you brought all this trouble on your own people, Lord? Why did you send me? Ever since I came to Pharaoh as your spokesman, he has been even more brutal to your people. And you have done nothing to rescue them!"

EXODUS 5:22–23 NLT

Praising God in Prayer

As the Hebrews reached the far side of the Red Sea and saw their enemies destroyed, their prayers turned to praise as they watched the promises God had shared with Moses come alive before their eyes. The Lord loves to hear the praises of His people. After all He has done for us, He deserves no less.

The Lord is my strength and song, and he is become my salvation: he is my God, and I will prepare him an habitation; my father's God, and I will exalt him.

EXODUS 15:2

"The Lord is my strength and song, and He has become my salvation; He is my God, and I will praise Him; my father's God, and I will exalt Him."

EXODUS 15:2 NKJV

A PROMISE TO LISTEN TO PRAYER

Following the giving of the Ten Commandments, God passed down more laws to Moses, rules that would help the Hebrew people live a holy life. Within those laws is God's promise to care for praying widows and orphans—to respond to their complaints against any who seek to take advantage of them. God hears the cry of the powerless, and His anger will rain down on those who harm them.

> *Ye shall not afflict any widow, or fatherless child. If thou afflict them in any wise, and they cry at all unto me, I will surely hear their cry; and my wrath shall wax hot, and I will kill you with the sword; and your wives shall be widows, and your children fatherless.*
>
> EXODUS 22:22–24

> *"Do not take advantage of the widow or the fatherless. If you do and they cry out to me, I will certainly hear their cry. My anger will be aroused, and I will kill you with the sword; your wives will become widows and your children fatherless."*
>
> EXODUS 22:22–24 NIV

MOSES PRAYS FOR ISRAEL

While Moses communed with God and received the Ten Commandments, his people became restless. They pushed Aaron to made an idol for them. God became extremely angry at His people, stating His desire to destroy them. But Moses prayed for the people, reminding God of the way He'd saved the nation by bringing them out of the land of Egypt. One man's intimate connection with God—and the powerful prayer it generates—can have far-reaching results. God decided not to destroy His people, and Moses returned to call them to repent and commit themselves to the Lord.

And Moses besought the LORD his God, and said, LORD, why doth thy wrath wax hot against thy people, which thou hast brought forth out of the land of Egypt with great power, and with a mighty hand?

EXODUS 32:11

But Moses sought the favor of the LORD his God. "LORD," he said, "why should your anger burn against your people, whom you brought out of Egypt with great power and a mighty hand?"

EXODUS 32:11 NLT

Prayer for God's Presence

When Moses knew that he and his people were headed for the Promised Land, he had a serious talk with God, making it clear that if the Lord would not go with them, the prophet didn't want to move a foot. Moses recognized the dangers of the journey and the huge impact on his nation—and unless God was with the people, their going would be disastrous. The rest of the account of Israel's move into the Promised Land shows what insight the prophet possessed.

> *And he said unto him, If thy presence go not with me, carry us not up hence.*
>
> EXODUS 33:15

> *Then Moses said to him, "If your Presence does not go with us, do not send us up from here."*
>
> EXODUS 33:15 NIV

PRAYER OR SACRIFICE?

Christians are accustomed to "simple" methods of forgiveness—in prayer we confess, depending on the sacrifice of Christ for our redemption, and God forgives. But in the Old Testament, God demanded a more complex way, one that impressed the seriousness of sin on His people. . .and it did not even seem to include prayer. The book of Leviticus prescribes animal sacrifices that prefigured Jesus' once-for-all-time sacrifice that made people right with God. Prayer is not directly mentioned in Leviticus, but can we imagine people came before God without having prayed about their wrongdoing?

> *And the priest shall make an atonement for his sin that he hath committed, and it shall be forgiven him.*
>
> LEVITICUS 4:35

> *Through this process, the priest will purify the people from their sin, making them right with the LORD, and they will be forgiven.*
>
> LEVITICUS 4:35 NLT

PRAYER WHEN UNDER ATTACK

Moses faced plenty of opposition in his lifetime, both from Israel's enemies and even his own countrymen. But perhaps no opposition was worse than that of his siblings, Aaron and Miriam, who became jealous of him and claimed they had as much right to be leaders of God's people. God made an object lesson of Miriam, punishing her rebellion by making her leprous. But despite her faithlessness toward Moses, her humble brother prayed for her healing. God in His mercy responded.

And Moses cried unto the LORD, saying, Heal her now, O God, I beseech thee.

NUMBERS 12:13

So Moses cried out to the LORD, "Please, God, heal her!"

NUMBERS 12:13 NIV

A PRAYER OF HUMILITY

God told Moses that—for a presumptuous sin committed before the people—he would not enter the Promised Land. So the prophet began to pray for his successor. Not every leader has this kind of humility, which certainly pleases God more than clinging to a ministry that He has declared over. Moses' prayer showed he cared more for his people than for his own importance.

> Let the LORD. . .set a man over the congregation, which may go out before them, and which may go in before them, and which may lead them out, and which may bring them in; that the congregation of the LORD be not as sheep which have no shepherd.
>
> NUMBERS 27:16–17

> "Please appoint a new man as leader for the community. Give them someone who will guide them wherever they go and will lead them into battle, so the community of the LORD will not be like sheep without a shepherd."
>
> NUMBERS 27:16–17 NLT

Prayer Denied

Moses desperately wanted to enter the Promised Land, and he asked God to let him. But God said no. That must have been a hard answer to hear, after Moses had been so faithful through so many experiences. But God allowed Moses at least a view of Canaan. He got to see the Promised Land from a distance, from the top of Mount Nebo, where he died.

> *I pray thee, let me go over, and see the good land that is beyond Jordan, that goodly mountain, and Lebanon.*
>
> DEUTERONOMY 3:25

> *"Let me go over and see the good land beyond the Jordan—that fine hill country and Lebanon."*
>
> DEUTERONOMY 3:25 NIV

Prayer for Past Help

Before God's people entered the Promised Land, He gave them some instructions. When they saw the firstfruits of their newly acquired land, they were to remember the past and give God thanks for their salvation from Egypt. He had enabled them to leave so much sorrow behind and gain so many blessings that it was only right to acknowledge Him. God wanted His people to remember the times they had called out to Him for help and He had responded.

> *And when we cried unto the LORD God of our fathers, the LORD heard our voice, and looked on our affliction, and our labour, and our oppression.*
>
> DEUTERONOMY 26:7

> *We cried out to the LORD, the God of our ancestors. He heard our cries and saw our hardship, toil, and oppression.*
>
> DEUTERONOMY 26:7 NLT

PRAYER AS PRAISE OF GOD

Can believers pray for long without bursting into praise? Those who know God must exalt Him and His works, as Moses did in his final appearance before the people of Israel. God's greatness underlies all He has done for His people, both in the Old and New Testaments.

> *I will publish the name of the LORD: ascribe ye greatness unto our God.*
>
> DEUTERONOMY 32:3

> *I will proclaim the name of the LORD. Oh, praise the greatness of our God!*
>
> DEUTERONOMY 32:3 NIV

A PRAYER OF DESPERATION

With a single battle lost, Joshua despaired. He feared God was letting him and his people down. But in his doubt Joshua turned immediately to prayer. God told the new leader this defeat was only a temporary setback because sin had entered the Israelites' camp. This episode shows that desperation does not need to be the end of any believer's story, because God is always there and He never fails.

And Joshua said, Alas, O LORD God, wherefore hast thou at all brought this people over Jordan, to deliver us into the hand of the Amorites, to destroy us? would to God we had been content, and dwelt on the other side Jordan!

JOSHUA 7:7

And Joshua said, "Alas, Sovereign LORD, why did you ever bring this people across the Jordan to deliver us into the hands of the Amorites to destroy us? If only we had been content to stay on the other side of the Jordan!"

JOSHUA 7:7 NIV

SLOW PRAYERS

It apparently took the Israelites twenty years to ask God to intervene in their ongoing oppression by Jabin, king of Canaan. When they did call out for God's help, He acted, won the battle, and freed His people. How much sooner could they have had God's help, if only they'd asked?

> *And the children of Israel cried unto the LORD: for he [the king of Canaan] had nine hundred chariots of iron; and twenty years he mightily oppressed the children of Israel.*
>
> JUDGES 4:3

> *And the children of Israel cried out to the LORD; for Jabin had nine hundred chariots of iron, and for twenty years he had harshly oppressed the children of Israel.*
>
> JUDGES 4:3 NKJV

PRAYER AND DISOBEDIENCE

After eighteen years of oppression by neighboring peoples, the Israelites recognized their sin of idolatry and went to God, asking for His help. At first He refused their request, reminding them how often He'd saved them before and how they'd still become idolaters. They should call on their pagan gods! But once the people showed Him their serious intent by obedience, God's heart turned—and He gave them the help they needed.

And the children of Israel said unto the
Lord, We have sinned: do thou unto us
whatsoever seemeth good unto thee; deliver
us only, we pray thee, this day. And they put
away the strange gods from among them,
and served the Lord: and his soul was
grieved for the misery of Israel.

JUDGES 10:15–16

But the Israelites said to the Lord, "We
have sinned. Do with us whatever you
think best, but please rescue us now." Then
they got rid of the foreign gods among them
and served the Lord. And he could bear
Israel's misery no longer.

JUDGES 10:15–16 NIV

AN ANSWER TO PRAYER

Though scripture does not record any prayers of Naomi, this verse certainly seems like an answer to prayer: Ruth refused to leave her widowed mother-in-law alone on her trip back to her homeland of Judah. Sometimes the Bible does not give us the words believers prayed, but we can still see God's hand working out the needs of those who love Him.

And Ruth said, Intreat me not to leave thee, or to return from following after thee: for whither thou goest, I will go; and where thou lodgest, I will lodge: thy people shall be my people, and thy God my God.

RUTH 1:16

But Ruth replied, "Don't urge me to leave you or to turn back from you. Where you go I will go, and where you stay I will stay. Your people will be my people and your God my God."

RUTH 1:16 NIV

MISUNDERSTOOD PRAYER

Silent in her praying, Hannah was misunderstood by Eli the priest. Though her lips moved, she was not praying out loud. Others at Shiloh probably worshipped noisily, but this barren woman kept her request between herself and God. Eli, who should have known better, was quick to judge, but God was not. He gave Hannah the request of her heart—a son who would become the prophet Samuel.

Hannah, she spake in her heart; only her lips moved, but her voice was not heard: therefore Eli thought she had been drunken. And Eli said unto her, How long wilt thou be drunken? put away thy wine from thee.

1 SAMUEL 1:13–14

Hannah was praying in her heart, and her lips were moving but her voice was not heard. Eli thought she was drunk and said to her, "How long are you going to stay drunk? Put away your wine."

1 SAMUEL 1:13–14 NIV

PRAYER FOR GOD'S WISDOM

God had clearly called Samuel to anoint a new king, but the prophet knew the current king, Saul, was not going to like that. Did God really expect him to put his life in jeopardy? Samuel asked God for a solution and got it immediately. The Lord protected His prophet by giving him another job: to make a sacrifice. In a dangerous place, God's wisdom did not fail the prophet—all Samuel had to do was bring his concern before the Lord.

> *And Samuel said, How can I go? if Saul hear it, he will kill me. And the Lord said, Take an heifer with thee, and say, I am come to sacrifice to the Lord.*
>
> 1 Samuel 16:2

> *But Samuel asked, "How can I do that? If Saul hears about it, he will kill me."*
> *"Take a heifer with you," the Lord replied, "and say that you have come to make a sacrifice to the Lord."*
>
> 1 Samuel 16:2 nlt

Prayer for Wisdom in Trouble

David, running for his life from the murderous King Saul, found relative safety in the land of the enemy Philistines. David and his men even served with the Philistine military, raiding the settlements of other people groups. One time, though, when David's soldiers returned to their home base at Ziklag, they found that their families had been captured by the Amalekites. His angry men wanted to kill David, but the endangered leader didn't rush into action. Instead he asked God what to do and received His wisdom.

And David enquired at the Lord, saying, Shall I pursue after this troop? shall I overtake them? And he answered him, Pursue: for thou shalt surely overtake them, and without fail recover all.

1 Samuel 30:8

And David inquired of the Lord, "Shall I pursue this raiding party? Will I overtake them?"

"Pursue them," he answered. "You will certainly overtake them and succeed in the rescue."

1 Samuel 30:8 niv

Prayer for Good Timing

When the Philistines learned that David had been anointed the next king of Israel, they threatened war against him and his men twice. Each time, David prayed about going into battle. The first time, God said, "Go, for I will surely deliver the Philistines into your hands" (2 Samuel 5:19 NIV). The second time, God's answer was to wait for His timing.

> *And let it be, when thou hearest the sound*
> *of a going in the tops of the mulberry trees,*
> *that then thou shalt bestir thyself: for then*
> *shall the LORD go out before thee, to smite*
> *the host of the Philistines.*
>
> 2 SAMUEL 5:24

> *"As soon as you hear the sound of marching*
> *in the tops of the poplar trees, move quickly,*
> *because that will mean the LORD has gone*
> *out in front of you to strike the Philistine*
> *army."*
>
> 2 SAMUEL 5:24 NIV

A Humble Prayer

When David's throne was finally secure and his kingdom peaceful, the one-time shepherd felt humbled by all God had done for him. So David worshipped God in prayer. Humbly, the king understood that it was not his own abilities that had made him great but the leading of God, who had brought him to this place.

> *Then went king David in, and sat before the LORD, and he said, Who am I, O Lord GOD? and what is my house, that thou hast brought me hitherto?*
>
> 2 SAMUEL 7:18

> *Then King David went in and sat before the LORD, and he said: "Who am I, Sovereign LORD, and what is my family, that you have brought me this far?"*
>
> 2 SAMUEL 7:18 NIV

A King's Confession

Despite the doubts of his military commander, Joab, King David wanted to count his people and find out how many fighting men were in his land. Afterwards, the king recognized the sin of his action—he was trusting his own power rather than God's. So David repented. God gave the king three options of punishment: famine, pursuit by his enemies, or plague. David chose the three-day plague, trusting in God's mercy. Israel suffered as seventy thousand people died. But as the "death angel" neared Jerusalem, David pleaded with God that the people should not be punished while his own household was safe. God stayed His hand.

And David spake unto the Lord when he saw the angel that smote the people, and said, Lo, I have sinned, and I have done wickedly: but these sheep, what have they done? let thine hand, I pray thee, be against me, and against my father's house.

2 Samuel 24:17

When David saw the angel, he said to the Lord, "I am the one who has sinned and done wrong! But these people are as innocent as sheep—what have they done? Let your anger fall against me and my family."

2 Samuel 24:17 NLT

WISE PRAYER

After David died, God came to Solomon and asked what He could give the new king. The wise, prayerful words that follow were Solomon's answer. But even the wisest man has weaknesses, and David's son was far from perfect. The same man who asked for the Lord's wisdom ultimately worshipped false gods. Real, heartfelt prayer must be a daily occurrence in the believer's life.

> *Give therefore thy servant an understanding heart to judge thy people, that I may discern between good and bad: for who is able to judge this thy so great a people?*
>
> 1 KINGS 3:9

> *"So give your servant a discerning heart to govern your people and to distinguish between right and wrong. For who is able to govern this great people of yours?"*
>
> 1 KINGS 3:9 NIV

Prayer that God Would Be Known

Israel had once again wandered from faith in God when the prophet Elijah built an altar, flooded it and a sacrifice with water, and publicly called on the nation to return to the Lord. Following this prayer that announced the work of God and his prophet, the Lord set the sacrifice alight.

> *And it came to pass at the time of the offering of the evening sacrifice, that Elijah the prophet came near, and said, LORD God of Abraham, Isaac, and of Israel, let it be known this day that thou art God in Israel, and that I am thy servant, and that I have done all these things at thy word.*
>
> 1 KINGS 18:36

> *At the time of sacrifice, the prophet Elijah stepped forward and prayed: "LORD, the God of Abraham, Isaac and Israel, let it be known today that you are God in Israel and that I am your servant and have done all these things at your command."*
>
> 1 KINGS 18:36 NIV

Prayer for Clear Sight

The prophet Elisha had a servant who feared the Syrian troops that surrounded Dothan, the city the two men had entered. Knowing the young man's fear, Elisha prayed that God would let him see the spiritual protection all around them. Soon, the doubting servant caught a glimpse of God's unseen forces about the city.

And Elisha prayed, and said, Lord, I pray thee, open his eyes, that he may see. And the Lord opened the eyes of the young man; and he saw: and, behold, the mountain was full of horses and chariots of fire round about Elisha.

2 Kings 6:17

And Elisha prayed, "Open his eyes, Lord, so that he may see." Then the Lord opened the servant's eyes, and he looked and saw the hills full of horses and chariots of fire all around Elisha.

2 Kings 6:17 niv

PRAYER FOR DEFENSE

The Assyrian king Sennacherib and his troops threatened Jerusalem, but worse than that, they defied and belittled God. So Judah's King Hezekiah went to the Lord and prayed for God to intervene and show His own power to the nations. God quickly responded, killing thousands of Assyrians in the night. The rest of the enemy quietly left Jerusalem, and the city was saved.

> *Now therefore, O LORD our God, I beseech thee, save thou us out of his hand, that all the kingdoms of the earth may know that thou art the LORD God, even thou only.*
>
> 2 KINGS 19:19

> *"Now, LORD our God, deliver us from his hand, so that all the kingdoms of the earth may know that you alone, LORD, are God."*
>
> 2 KINGS 19:19 NIV

GOD HEARS SHORT PRAYERS TOO

Hezekiah heard from the prophet Isaiah that God was prepared to take his life. The faithful king prayed a fervent, short prayer, and before Isaiah could leave the palace, God turned him around with a new, hope-filled message for the king. God hears every prayer, even our shortest, most desperate ones.

> *Then he turned his face to the wall, and prayed unto the LORD, saying, I beseech thee, O LORD, remember now how I have walked before thee in truth and with a perfect heart, and have done that which is good in thy sight. And Hezekiah wept sore.*
> 2 KINGS 20:2–3

> *When Hezekiah heard this, he turned his face to the wall and prayed to the LORD, "Remember, O LORD, how I have always been faithful to you and have served you single-mindedly, always doing what pleases you." Then he broke down and wept bitterly.*
> 2 KINGS 20:2–3 NLT

Prayer for Blessing

An otherwise unknown Bible character named Jabez prayed for just about all the good things he could think of, and God answered him because his heart was in the right place. Praying with a clean heart, for the things God wants, can bring great blessing.

> *And Jabez called on the God of Israel, saying, Oh that thou wouldest bless me indeed, and enlarge my coast, and that thine hand might be with me, and that thou wouldest keep me from evil, that it may not grieve me! And God granted him that which he requested.*
>
> 1 Chronicles 4:10

> *Jabez cried out to the God of Israel, "Oh, that you would bless me and enlarge my territory! Let your hand be with me, and keep me from harm so that I will be free from pain." And God granted his request.*
>
> 1 Chronicles 4:10 NIV

TRUSTING PRAYERS

In the midst of battle, things weren't going well for the Jewish tribes that settled east of the Jordan River—the Reubenites, the Gadites, and half-tribe of Manasseh. But as they fought, they cried out to God in real need and trust. God answered, giving them victory in their battle. Prayers without trust are worthless, but sometimes God brings His people to desperation so that they will turn to Him wholeheartedly.

They cried to God in the battle, and he was intreated of them; because they put their trust in him.

1 CHRONICLES 5:20

They cried out to God during the battle, and he answered their prayer because they trusted in him.

1 CHRONICLES 5:20 NLT

PRAYER IN AFFLICTION

The Assyrians attacked and conquered Judah, and faithless King Manasseh was captured and humbled. In his pain, he finally sought the Lord. Manasseh's prayer began a spiritual life that was worth having.

*And when he [Manasseh] was in affliction,
he besought the LORD his God, and
humbled himself greatly before the God
of his fathers, and prayed unto him: and
he was intreated of him, and heard his
supplication, and brought him again to
Jerusalem into his kingdom. Then
Manasseh knew that the LORD he was God.*
                    2 CHRONICLES 33:12–13

*In his distress he [Manasseh] sought the
favor of the LORD his God and humbled
himself greatly before the God of his ancestors.
And when he prayed to him, the LORD
was moved by his entreaty and listened to
his plea; so he brought him back to Jerusalem
and to his kingdom. Then Manasseh knew
that the LORD is God.*
                    2 CHRONICLES 33:12–13 NIV

A Prayer of Desperate Trust

The exiled priest Ezra had told the Persian king Artaxerxes how powerful the God of Israel was, so the king planned to return the Jews to their homeland. How then could Ezra ask the ruler to provide soldiers to protect the people on the long walk home? Instead, the fearful Jews desperately placed their trust in God, praying for His protection on the journey.

> *For I was ashamed to require of the king a band of soldiers and horsemen to help us against the enemy in the way: because we had spoken unto the king, saying, The hand of our God is upon all them for good that seek him; but his power and his wrath is against all them that forsake him. So we fasted and besought our God for this: and he was intreated of us.*
>
> EZRA 8:22–23

> *I was ashamed to ask the king for soldiers and horsemen to protect us from enemies on the road, because we had told the king, "The gracious hand of our God is on everyone who looks to him, but his great anger is against all who forsake him." So we fasted and petitioned our God about this, and he answered our prayer.*
>
> EZRA 8:22–23 NIV

Prayer for a Sinful Nation

After returning from exile, Ezra heard reports that the Jews who had remained in the land had intermarried with pagans and turned from God. In embarrassment, he went to the Lord in prayer, detailing the people's sorry history and asking forgiveness.

And at the evening sacrifice I arose up from my heaviness; and having rent my garment and my mantle, I fell upon my knees, and spread out my hands unto the LORD my God, and said, O my God, I am ashamed and blush to lift up my face to thee, my God: for our iniquities are increased over our head, and our trespass is grown up unto the heavens.

EZRA 9:5–6

Then, at the evening sacrifice, I rose from my self-abasement, with my tunic and cloak torn, and fell on my knees with my hands spread out to the LORD my God and prayed: "I am too ashamed and disgraced, my God, to lift up my face to you, because our sins are higher than our heads and our guilt has reached to the heavens."

EZRA 9:5–6 NIV

PRAYER FOR GOD'S INFLUENCE OVER OTHERS

Nehemiah, Jewish cupbearer to the Persian king, Artaxerxes, heard news of the distress of Jerusalem and wanted to help. But to go to Jerusalem, he needed the permission of the powerful Persian ruler. Nehemiah went to God in prayer, and God made a way for him to serve his people instead of a foreign king.

O LORD, I beseech thee, let now thine ear be attentive to the prayer of thy servant, and to the prayer of thy servants, who desire to fear thy name: and prosper, I pray thee, thy servant this day, and grant him mercy in the sight of this man. For I was the king's cupbearer.

NEHEMIAH 1:11

"Lord, let your ear be attentive to the prayer of this your servant and to the prayer of your servants who delight in revering your name. Give your servant success today by granting him favor in the presence of this man." I was cupbearer to the king.

NEHEMIAH 1:11 NIV

CONFESSION IN PRAYER

As the temple in Jerusalem was being refurbished, the leaders of Israel read the Law to all the people. These Israelites understood how far they had strayed from God's will by intermarrying with unbelievers. Once they knew how God desired them to live, they responded by freely confessing their failures and worshipping Him.

> *And the seed of Israel separated themselves*
> *from all strangers, and stood and confessed*
> *their sins, and the iniquities of their fathers.*
> *And they stood up in their place, and read*
> *in the book of the law of the LORD their*
> *God one fourth part of the day; and another*
> *fourth part they confessed, and worshipped*
> *the LORD their God.*
>
> NEHEMIAH 9:2–3

> *Those of Israelite descent had separated*
> *themselves from all foreigners. They stood in*
> *their places and confessed their sins and the*
> *sins of their ancestors. They stood where they*
> *were and read from the Book of the Law of*
> *the LORD their God for a quarter of the day,*
> *and spent another quarter in confession and*
> *in worshiping the LORD their God.*
>
> NEHEMIAH 9:2–3 NIV

Prayer in Danger

The book of Esther has no specific mention of God or prayer, yet His hand is obvious throughout. Warned of the imminent destruction of the Jews, Esther promised her cousin Mordecai that she and her women would fast before she took the dangerous step of going to the king unbidden. Since prayer and fasting are so closely connected in scripture, can we doubt that Esther also prayed before she risked her life?

> *Go, gather together all the Jews that are present in Shushan, and fast ye for me, and neither eat nor drink three days, night or day: I also and my maidens will fast likewise; and so will I go in unto the king, which is not according to the law: and if I perish, I perish.*

> ESTHER 4:16

> *"Go and gather together all the Jews of Susa and fast for me. Do not eat or drink for three days, night or day. My maids and I will do the same. And then, though it is against the law, I will go in to see the king. If I must die, I must die."*

> ESTHER 4:16 NLT

PRAYER IN TROUBLE

In one fell swoop, at the instigation of Satan, Job lost his flocks, his cattle, and his ten children. Yet this remarkable man still praised God and did not say anything against Him. In trouble, those who love God can turn to Him in prayer, knowing He can turn around even our worst disasters.

> *And [Job] said, Naked came I out of my mother's womb, and naked shall I return thither: the LORD gave, and the LORD hath taken away; blessed be the name of the LORD. In all this Job sinned not, nor charged God foolishly.*
>
> JOB 1:21–22

> *And [Job] said: "Naked I came from my mother's womb, and naked I will depart. The LORD gave and the LORD has taken away; may the name of the LORD be praised." In all this, Job did not sin by charging God with wrongdoing.*
>
> JOB 1:21–22 NIV

PRAYER AND SEEING GOD

Though Job knew God all along, when the Lord confronted him and showed His power, the faithful man was completely humbled, repenting of his earlier thoughts and words. It was as if Job had heard about God but never really knew Him. Meeting God in all His power, Job suddenly realized how little he had appreciated and understood the Lord. And he said so to God.

> *I have heard of thee by the hearing of the ear: but now mine eye seeth thee. Wherefore I abhor myself, and repent in dust and ashes.*
>
> JOB 42:5–6

> *"My ears had heard of you but now my eyes have seen you. Therefore I despise myself and repent in dust and ashes."*
>
> JOB 42:5–6 NIV

PRAYER FOR PAINFUL FRIENDS

Job's three friends had foolishly accused him of all kinds of wrongdoing. But when God made Himself known, standing up for Job against his accusers, Job willingly prayed for them. As he prayed, God made it a turning point in his life.

And the LORD turned the captivity of Job,
when he prayed for his friends: also the
LORD gave Job twice as much as he had
before.

JOB 42:10

After Job had prayed for his friends, the
LORD restored his fortunes and gave him
twice as much as he had before.

JOB 42:10 NIV

PRAYER ABOUT ENEMIES

Surrounded by enemies who claimed that the Lord
would never help him, King David turned to God
in prayer. As he poured out his heart, David began
to understand that his enemies were wrong. God
was the solution and would still help him.

Lord, how are they increased that trouble
me! many are they that rise up against me.

PSALM 3:1

LORD, how many are my foes! How many
rise up against me!

PSALM 3:1 NIV

PRAYER TO A DISTANT GOD

Both King David and Jesus knew what it was to experience a God who felt distant. David cried out to his Lord with these words, and Jesus quoted them on the cross. In both cases the feelings of being forsaken were not the end of the story. Neither David nor Jesus were abandoned by God.

> *My God, my God, why hast thou forsaken me? why art thou so far from helping me, and from the words of my roaring?*
>
> PSALM 22:1

> *My God, my God, why have you abandoned me? Why are you so far away when I groan for help?*
>
> PSALM 22:1 NLT

A PRAYER OF GOD'S FAITHFULNESS

Though King David doubted that God had heard his prayers in great troubles, he discovered, down the road, that God *had* been listening. The Lord's response was not as immediate as the king might have wished, but God's faithful nature had not changed. When David realized that truth, he praised God for it.

For I said in my haste, I am cut off from
before thine eyes: nevertheless thou heardest
the voice of my supplications when I cried
unto thee.

PSALM 31:22

In my alarm I said, "I am cut off from your
sight!" Yet you heard my cry for mercy when
I called to you for help.

PSALM 31:22 NIV

PRAISE AS TESTIMONY

Praise is a very special kind of prayer that thanks God for what He's done. David recognized the importance of praise not only in his own spiritual life, but also as a testimony to God's faithfulness.

And he hath put a new song in my mouth,
even praise unto our God: many shall see it,
and fear, and shall trust in the LORD.

PSALM 40:3

He put a new song in my mouth, a hymn of
praise to our God. Many will see and fear
the LORD and put their trust in him.

PSALM 40:3 NIV

DESIRING GOD

The Jewish musicians known as the sons of Korah recognized that loving God is not simply a nice extra. Those who believe in God need Him as much as a deer needs water to live. Living without God is like dwelling in a parched land.

> *As the hart panteth after the water brooks,*
> *so panteth my soul after thee, O God.*
>
> PSALM 42:1

> *As the deer pants for streams of water, so my*
> *soul pants for you, my God.*
>
> PSALM 42:1 NIV

PRAYER IN WRONGDOING

After his adultery with Bathsheba, David recognized that he had not only wronged people. He had really offended God, whose nature abhorred the lust, adultery, and murder that David committed. No longer did the king attempt to avoid his sin—he placed his guilt squarely before God, seeking forgiveness.

> *Against thee, thee only, have I sinned, and*
> *done this evil in thy sight: that thou mightest*
> *be justified when thou speakest, and be*
> *clear when thou judgest.*
>
> PSALM 51:4

*Against you, you only, have I sinned and
done what is evil in your sight; so you are
right in your verdict and justified when you
judge.*

PSALM 51:4 NIV

COMPLAINING PRAYER

It's not something to make a habit of, but sometimes we can even raise complaints in our prayers.
Psalm writers and prophets occasionally voiced
their unhappiness, often with God Himself, not
understanding why He seemed distant or allowed
wicked people to prevail. God can handle our
honest frustration—but like the biblical writers,
we should ultimately remind ourselves of His
goodness and come back to praise: "But I will
trust in thee" (Psalm 55:23).

*Give ear to my prayer, O God; and hide
not thyself from my supplication. Attend
unto me, and hear me: I mourn in my
complaint, and make a noise.*

PSALM 55:1–2

*Listen to my prayer, O God, do not ignore
my plea; hear me and answer me. My
thoughts trouble me and I am distraught.*

PSALM 55:1–2 NIV

PRAYER ABOUT GOD'S STEADFASTNESS

No matter where they go, believers dwell in God, who existed before creation. Though the world and mankind are frail and easily destroyed, the One who created them lasts forever and is worthy of trust. When nothing seems secure, God always will be.

Lord, thou hast been our dwelling place in all generations. Before the mountains were brought forth, or ever thou hadst formed the earth and the world, even from everlasting to everlasting, thou art God.

PSALM 90:1–2

Lord, you have been our dwelling place throughout all generations. Before the mountains were born or you brought forth the whole world, from everlasting to everlasting you are God.

PSALM 90:1–2 NIV

APPRECIATING GOD'S UNDERSTANDING

David's life had been terribly complicated as he sought to obey God and serve as Israel's king. From the psalms he wrote, it's clear that he often felt lonely and far from others. But Psalm 139 shows that even when he felt estranged from others, he had learned that God knew everything that was happening in his life. Nothing about David was outside of God's understanding.

Thou knowest my downsitting and mine uprising, thou understandest my thought afar off.

PSALM 139:2

You know when I sit and when I rise; you perceive my thoughts from afar.

PSALM 139:2 NIV

PRAISE FOR A WONDERFUL GOD

It doesn't take much to find things to praise God for, as the prophet Isaiah discovered. He looked at what God had done for himself and his countrymen—good things that God had planned all along—and began to praise His name.

> *O Lord, thou art my God; I will exalt thee, I will praise thy name; for thou hast done wonderful things.*
>
> ISAIAH 25:1

> *LORD, you are my God; I will exalt you and praise your name, for in perfect faithfulness you have done wonderful things.*
>
> ISAIAH 25:1 NIV

PRAYER TO THE POTTER

Just as a potter puts clay onto his wheel to create a bowl, a cup, or some other item, God makes human lives with a wonderful delicacy. And just as the potter who forms an object can refashion or remake it, God can do as He pleases with believers' lives.

> *But now, O LORD, thou art our father; we are the clay, and thou our potter; and we all are the work of thy hand.*
>
> ISAIAH 64:8

Yet you, LORD, are our Father. We are the
clay, you are the potter; we are all the work
of your hand.

ISAIAH 64:8 NIV

PRAYER—A TWO-WAY STREET

Prayer is not one-sided; God speaks back to His people. One day God approached the prophet Jeremiah to say that the people had turned from Him. Jeremiah's job was to carry that message to the nation. When His people are open to it, God will speak to them and direct them into His way. Then they can turn their lives once again to the paths God has in mind.

Hath a nation changed their gods, which
are yet no gods? but my people have changed
their glory for that which doth not profit.

JEREMIAH 2:11

Has a nation ever changed its gods? (Yet
they are not gods at all.) But my people
have exchanged their glorious God for
worthless idols.

JEREMIAH 2:11 NIV

PRAYER FORBIDDEN

Israel had become so disobedient and rebellious that God gave Jeremiah an unusual message: he was forbidden to pray for the nation. Though God had reached out to the people constantly, Israel looked to idols instead. So God gave them what they seemed to want.

> *Therefore pray not thou for this people, neither lift up cry nor prayer for them, neither make intercession to me: for I will not hear thee.*
>
> JEREMIAH 7:16

> *"So do not pray for this people nor offer any plea or petition for them; do not plead with me, for I will not listen to you."*
>
> JEREMIAH 7:16 NIV

Prayer in Times of Suffering

Jeremiah felt overwhelmed by the suffering his prophetic calling brought to him. So he called out to God. Despite the troubles in the prophet's life, Jeremiah trusted in the Lord, who had always been faithful to him. God responded with a call for the prophet to repent from his complaining (see Jeremiah 15:19).

O LORD, thou knowest: remember me, and visit me, and revenge me of my persecutors; take me not away in thy longsuffering: know that for thy sake I have suffered rebuke.

JEREMIAH 15:15

LORD, you understand; remember me and care for me. Avenge me on my persecutors. You are long-suffering—do not take me away; think of how I suffer reproach for your sake.

JEREMIAH 15:15 NIV

PRAYER FOR HEALING

While God gave His prophet the message of judgment on Judah, Jeremiah felt convicted of his own sinfulness and need for healing. Whom should he go to but the Lord for both physical and spiritual healing?

Heal me, O LORD, and I shall be healed; save me, and I shall be saved: for thou art my praise.

JEREMIAH 17:14

O LORD, if you heal me, I will be truly healed; if you save me, I will be truly saved. My praises are for you alone!

JEREMIAH 17:14 NLT

PRAYER PROMISE

God has a short, sweet, powerful promise for our prayers: when our whole hearts reach out to Him, desiring to know Him, He will be found. God doesn't want to be distant from His people, but He never encourages half-hearted prayers. Those who are serious about knowing God will find He draws near. But people who can't decide to really walk in His ways may find God elusive. A human heart that really searches for Him will always touch His heart.

*And ye shall seek me, and find me, when ye
shall search for me with all your heart.*

JEREMIAH 29:13

*"You will seek me and find me when you
seek me with all your heart."*

JEREMIAH 29:13 NIV

A Prayer of Trust

As the Babylonians threatened Jerusalem, Jeremiah still recognized where his trust had to be—and he offered praise to the Lord. Though men would attack or fail Jeremiah, he knew that the Lord who created all things was still in charge of the nations. As He had saved and blessed His people before, He would do so again (see Jeremiah 32:21–22).

*Ah Lord GOD! behold, thou hast made the
heaven and the earth by thy great power
and stretched out arm, and there is nothing
too hard for thee.*

JEREMIAH 32:17

*"Ah, Sovereign LORD, you have made the
heavens and the earth by your great power
and outstretched arm. Nothing is too hard
for you."*

JEREMIAH 32:17 NIV

Prayer When God Is Distant

The prophet Jeremiah grieved over the destruction of his city and the waywardness of his people. God no longer even seemed to answer prayer. But as Jeremiah pursued God, he recognized that all he had to do was wait for the Lord (see Lamentations 3:24). God had never deserted him.

> *Also when I cry and shout, he shutteth out my prayer. . . . [But] it is of the LORD's mercies that we are not consumed, because his compassions fail not.*
>
> LAMENTATIONS 3:8, 22

> *Even when I call out or cry for help, he shuts out my prayer. . . . [But] because of the LORD's great love we are not consumed, for his compassions never fail.*
>
> LAMENTATIONS 3:8, 22 NIV

PRAYER FOR SANCTUARY

In a vision, Ezekiel saw the people of Judah destroyed by God's command, and the prophet cried out to God for them. Though they had fallen far from God, Ezekiel still had compassion. Though God did not seem inclined to ease their plight, in Ezekiel 11:16 He promised that even though the people would go to foreign lands, He would be their sanctuary.

And it came to pass, while they were slaying them, and I was left, that I fell upon my face, and cried, and said, Ah Lord GOD! wilt thou destroy all the residue of Israel in thy pouring out of thy fury upon Jerusalem?

EZEKIEL 9:8

While they were killing and I was left alone, I fell facedown, crying out, "Alas, Sovereign LORD! Are you going to destroy the entire remnant of Israel in this outpouring of your wrath on Jerusalem?"

EZEKIEL 9:8 NIV

HELP IN PRAYER

When King Nebuchadnezzar had a dream, he ordered his counselors to tell him what that dream was and what it meant. If they could not, he would put them to death. Daniel immediately went to his faithful prayer partners, who asked that God would give their friend the knowledge and protection he needed.

> *Then Daniel went to his house, and made the thing known to Hananiah, Mishael, and Azariah, his companions: That they would desire mercies of the God of heaven concerning this secret; that Daniel and his fellows should not perish with the rest of the wise men of Babylon.*
>
> DANIEL 2:17–18

> *Then Daniel returned to his house and explained the matter to his friends Hananiah, Mishael and Azariah. He urged them to plead for mercy from the God of heaven concerning this mystery, so that he and his friends might not be executed with the rest of the wise men of Babylon.*
>
> DANIEL 2:17–18 NIV

BRAVERY IN PRAYER

When King Darius made a decree that for thirty days no one should pray to anyone but him, his counselor Daniel did not stand down. Bravely, Daniel continued his prayers to the true God in front of everyone. As a result, the prophet became a testimony to God's power when the Lord saved him from being harmed in a den full of lions.

> *Now when Daniel knew that the writing was signed, he went into his house; and his windows being open in his chamber toward Jerusalem, he kneeled upon his knees three times a day, and prayed, and gave thanks before his God, as he did aforetime.*
>
> DANIEL 6:10

> *Now when Daniel learned that the decree had been published, he went home to his upstairs room where the windows opened toward Jerusalem. Three times a day he got down on his knees and prayed, giving thanks to his God, just as he had done before.*
>
> DANIEL 6:10 NIV

FAITHLESS PRAYER

Though Israel was faithless to God, the nation *claimed* to know Him. Yet the people did not recognize that their prayers were worthless because they would not repent and truly follow God. So God sent enemies to pursue them. The Lord will not answer the false prayers of those who do not serve Him.

> *Israel shall cry unto me, My God, we know thee. Israel hath cast off the thing that is good: the enemy shall pursue him.*
>
> HOSEA 8:2–3

> *Israel cries out to me, "Our God, we acknowledge you!" But Israel has rejected what is good; an enemy will pursue him.*
>
> HOSEA 8:2–3 NIV

PRAYER IN THE MIDDLE OF DISASTER

As judgment fell upon the land because of Judah's unfaithfulness, Joel called out to God, the Creator of the earth, to intervene and stop the destruction of the pastures, fields, and woodlands—all the elements of the earth that supported people's needs. Only God could end the disaster and lift His judgment from His unfaithful people.

O LORD, to thee will I cry: for the fire hath
devoured the pastures of the wilderness, and
the flame hath burned all the trees of the field.
JOEL 1:19

LORD, help us! The fire has consumed
the wilderness pastures, and flames have
burned up all the trees.
JOEL 1:19 NLT

SALVATION FROM DESTRUCTION

Twice in Amos 7:1–4 God showed the prophet
that He would destroy Israel, and the prophet
begged Him to forgive His rebellious but frail
people. Though God relented and did not use lo-
custs or fire to ruin the land, He did plan to send
Israel into exile.

And it came to pass, that when they had made
an end of eating the grass of the land, then I
said, O Lord GOD, forgive, I beseech thee: by
whom shall Jacob arise? for he is small.
AMOS 7:2

When they had stripped the land clean,
I cried out, "Sovereign LORD, forgive!
How can Jacob survive? He is so small!"
AMOS 7:2 NIV

PRAYER FOR HELP

After three days in the belly of a fish, the prophet Jonah repented for his disobedience of God's command to take a message to Nineveh. Even from such an unlikely place as Jonah found himself, God heard and quickly responded to the prophet's cry for help.

> *I cried by reason of mine affliction unto the LORD, and he heard me; out of the belly of hell cried I, and thou heardest my voice.*
>
> JONAH 2:2

> *"In my distress I called to the LORD, and he answered me. From deep in the realm of the dead I called for help, and you listened to my cry."*
>
> JONAH 2:2 NIV

PRAYER OF A PEOPLE

Jonah ultimately obeyed God, going to Nineveh to warn the city of the destruction the Lord had planned for them. When the king heard the message, he called on everyone in the nation to repent. The people obeyed his command, prayed and turned from evil, and were saved.

> *But let man and beast be covered with sackcloth, and cry mightily unto God: yea, let them turn every one from his evil way, and from the violence that is in their hands.*
>
> JONAH 3:8

> *"People and animals alike must wear garments of mourning, and everyone must pray earnestly to God. They must turn from their evil ways and stop all their violence."*
>
> JONAH 3:8 NLT

PRAYER OF DESPAIR

When Jonah heard that the people of Nineveh had repented and that God had forgiven them, he was terribly unhappy. The Ninevites were enemies of his people, and Jonah had preached to them only at God's insistence. So he asked God to let him die. God had saved Israel's enemies through his own testimony—now would they destroy Jonah's land?

> *Therefore now, O LORD, take, I beseech thee, my life from me; for it is better for me to die than to live.*
>
> JONAH 4:3

> *"Now, LORD, take away my life, for it is better for me to die than to live."*
>
> JONAH 4:3 NIV

PRAYERS OF THE FAITHLESS UNANSWERED

Unfaithful prophets and seers had told Micah that God would not send His people into exile, and they spread this false message through the land of Judah. But they did not get the response they expected from God. When Micah gave them bad news, he was right—exile was in their future. Because these spiritual leaders would not listen to God's true prophet, God was silent when they prayed.

> *Then shall the seers be ashamed, and the diviners confounded: yea, they shall all cover their lips; for there is no answer of God.*
>
> MICAH 3:7

> *"The seers will be ashamed and the diviners disgraced. They will all cover their faces because there is no answer from God."*
>
> MICAH 3:7 NIV

Waiting in Prayer

When Judah began to feel the pinch of God's judgment, the people were miserable. Micah declared the only solution: Wait on God, hoping in Him.

> *Therefore I will look unto the LORD; I will wait for the God of my salvation: my God will hear me.*
>
> MICAH 7:7

> *But as for me, I watch in hope for the LORD, I wait for God my Savior; my God will hear me.*
>
> MICAH 7:7 NIV

Prayer about the Wicked

Confused, the prophet Habakkuk questioned God about the wickedness he saw all about him. Why did a pure God not judge these impure people? In response, God promised He would not fail, even if He at times seemed slow (Habakkuk 2:3). God's timeline was not Habakkuk's, but His nature had not changed—and justice would be done.

> *Thou art of purer eyes than to behold evil, and canst not look on iniquity: wherefore lookest thou upon them that deal treacherously, and holdest thy tongue when the*

*wicked devoureth the man that is more
righteous than he?*

HABAKKUK 1:13

*Your eyes are too pure to look on evil; you
cannot tolerate wrongdoing. Why then do
you tolerate the treacherous? Why are you
silent while the wicked swallow up those
more righteous than themselves?*

HABAKKUK 1:13 NIV

PRAYER FOR MERCY

After questioning God's actions, Habakkuk came
to understand the awesome Lord he served. The
prophet humbled himself before God, asking only
for mercy for the fears that caused his spiritual
failure.

*O LORD, I have heard thy speech, and was
afraid: O LORD, revive thy work in the
midst of the years, in the midst of the years
make known; in wrath remember mercy.*

HABAKKUK 3:2

*LORD, I have heard of your fame; I stand
in awe of your deeds, LORD. Repeat them in
our day, in our time make them known; in
wrath remember mercy.*

HABAKKUK 3:2 NIV

WORSHIP AND PRAYER

Though prayer is not specifically mentioned in this verse, it is always a part of worship. One day, when God brings His people back together as a nation, they will worship Him together.

From beyond the rivers of Ethiopia my suppliants, even the daughter of my dispersed, shall bring mine offering.
ZEPHANIAH 3:10

"From beyond the rivers of Cush my worshipers, my scattered people, will bring me offerings."
ZEPHANIAH 3:10 NIV

A PLACE OF PRAYER

Though God's people had returned to Jerusalem to rebuild the temple, they had delayed starting the project. So God encouraged them to begin the construction. Though He was dealing with a prayerless people, the Lord intended to have a place of prayer and worship, and to lead His people into glorifying Him. Prayerlessness should not last forever among God's people.

Thus saith the LORD of hosts; Consider your ways. Go up to the mountain, and bring wood, and build the house; and I will take pleasure in it, and I will be glorified, saith the LORD.

HAGGAI 1:7–8

"This is what the LORD of Heaven's Armies says: Look at what's happening to you! Now go up into the hills, bring down timber, and rebuild my house. Then I will take pleasure in it and be honored, says the LORD."

HAGGAI 1:7–8 NLT

WORSHIP IN DISCOURAGEMENT

As the Jewish people struggled to rebuild the temple, God sent them promises that probably seemed impossible: one day joy would be their portion from God, and they and their children would rejoice. Could any joy come without prayer and praise?

> *And they of Ephraim shall be like a mighty man, and their heart shall rejoice as through wine: yea, their children shall see it, and be glad; their heart shall rejoice in the LORD.*
>
> ZECHARIAH 10:7

> *The Ephraimites will become like warriors, and their hearts will be glad as with wine. Their children will see it and be joyful; their hearts will rejoice in the LORD.*
>
> ZECHARIAH 10:7 NIV

PRAYER AND ACTIONS

When is prayer not really prayer? When it is not followed by godly actions. Though God heard words of "prayer" from the people of Malachi's day, they did not please Him—because the people did not do good works. God never wants to hear empty words, but He delights in obedience from His people.

> Ye have wearied the LORD with your words.
> Yet ye say, Wherein have we wearied him?
> When ye say, Every one that doeth evil
> is good in the sight of the LORD, and he
> delighteth in them; or, Where is the God of
> judgment?
>
> MALACHI 2:17

> You have wearied the LORD with your
> words. "How have we wearied him?" you
> ask. By saying, "All who do evil are good in
> the eyes of the LORD, and he is pleased with
> them" or "Where is the God of justice?"
>
> MALACHI 2:17 NIV

A PRAYER THAT GOD OVERHEARS

Concerned about the state of their nation, a remnant of faithful Jews spoke to one another about their failings in God's eyes. Even though they weren't really praying, God heard their concerns. He honored them with a scroll of remembrance and promised to spare them.

Then they that feared the LORD spake often one to another: and the LORD hearkened, and heard it, and a book of remembrance was written before him for them that feared the LORD, and that thought upon his name.
                                    MALACHI 3:16

Then those who feared the LORD talked with each other, and the LORD listened and heard. A scroll of remembrance was written in his presence concerning those who feared the LORD and honored his name.
                                    MALACHI 3:16 NIV

PRIVATE PRAYERS

In this verse Jesus wasn't saying that Christians should avoid public prayer. He was telling His people that praying to get attention from others is not a good idea. Some Jews of Jesus' day would stand in public, seeming to address God but really trying just to make people think they were holy. God saw through that and called on believers to be honest with Him.

> *But thou, when thou prayest, enter into thy closet, and when thou hast shut thy door, pray to thy Father which is in secret; and thy Father which seeth in secret shall reward thee openly.*
>
> MATTHEW 6:6

> *"But when you pray, go into your room, close the door and pray to your Father, who is unseen. Then your Father, who sees what is done in secret, will reward you."*
>
> MATTHEW 6:6 NIV

PRAYER FOR DELIVERANCE FROM TEMPTATION

The end of the Lord's prayer is a reminder that God alone delivers us from the temptations that come from the hand of Satan. God, who is in charge of all things on this earth, has the power to keep us faithful, no matter how Satan attacks us.

And lead us not into temptation,
but deliver us from evil.

MATTHEW 6:13

"And don't let us yield to temptation,
but rescue us from the evil one."

MATTHEW 6:13 NLT

ASKING GOD IN PRAYER

Who else but God would give the faithful such an open door? Jesus calls us to ask God for all that we want and need—though we must ask wisely. But if we request things in accordance with His will, He will always answer.

Ask, and it shall be given you; seek, and
ye shall find; knock, and it shall be opened
unto you.

MATTHEW 7:7

"Ask and it will be given to you; seek and you will find; knock and the door will be opened to you."

MATTHEW 7:7 NIV

PRAYER FOR GOD'S WORKERS

Anyone who works in ministry will come to recognize that more workers are essential. Jesus told His disciples to ask God to provide workers to bring in the "harvest" of human souls. He will answer this prayer.

Then saith he unto his disciples, The harvest truly is plenteous, but the labourers are few. Pray ye therefore the Lord of the harvest, that he will send forth labourers into his harvest.

MATTHEW 9:37–38

Then he said to his disciples, "The harvest is plentiful but the workers are few. Ask the Lord of the harvest, therefore, to send out workers into his harvest field."

MATTHEW 9:37–38 NIV

Prayer for Salvation

Tossed about by boisterous wind and waves, Jesus' disciples huddled on a boat on the Sea of Galilee. All except Peter, that is. He had stepped out of the boat at Jesus' command and was walking on the water just like Jesus! But when the storm distracted him, Peter quickly began to sink and called out for salvation. Of course Jesus was with him immediately, showing Peter that he was always safe when his eyes were on the Lord.

> *But when he [Peter] saw the wind boisterous, he was afraid; and beginning to sink, he cried, saying, Lord, save me.*
> MATTHEW 14:30

> *But when he [Peter] saw the wind, he was afraid and, beginning to sink, cried out, "Lord, save me!"*
> MATTHEW 14:30 NIV

A COMMUNITY OF PRAYER

Amazingly, God tells us that when we gather together in prayer, He will answer. He will not ignore
the prayers of His people who faithfully gather. It
only takes a community of two people—joined
with God—to become a powerful prayer force.

Again I say unto you, That if two of you
shall agree on earth as touching any thing
that they shall ask, it shall be done for them
of my Father which is in heaven. For where
two or three are gathered together in my
name, there am I in the midst of them.
MATTHEW 18:19–20

"Again, truly I tell you that if two of you
on earth agree about anything they ask for,
it will be done for them by my Father in
heaven. For where two or three gather in
my name, there am I with them."
MATTHEW 18:19–20 NIV

Prayer for Children

If Jesus set an example of praying for children, we should certainly follow that example. Though His disciples callously tried to shoo the little ones away, Jesus insisted that they be allowed to come to Him. The Lord's prayers for the children were not recorded, but it's safe to assume He asked the Father for their salvation. As He had taught not long before, "Except ye be converted, and become as little children, ye shall not enter into the kingdom of heaven" (Matthew 18:3).

Then were there brought unto him little children, that he should put his hands on them, and pray: and the disciples rebuked them. But Jesus said, Suffer little children, and forbid them not, to come unto me: for of such is the kingdom of heaven.

MATTHEW 19:13–14

Then people brought little children to Jesus for him to place his hands on them and pray for them. But the disciples rebuked them. Jesus said, "Let the little children come to me, and do not hinder them, for the kingdom of heaven belongs to such as these."

MATTHEW 19:13–14 NIV

PRAYER FOR MERCY

During Jesus' ministry, two blind men worship-fully (yet noisily) begged Him for healing. The surrounding crowd rebuked them, but their need was so great that they would not stop asking for Jesus' compassion—which He gave to them.

And, behold, two blind men sitting by the way side, when they heard that Jesus passed by, cried out, saying, Have mercy on us, O Lord, thou son of David.

MATTHEW 20:30

Two blind men were sitting beside the road. When they heard that Jesus was coming that way, they began shouting, "Lord, Son of David, have mercy on us!"

MATTHEW 20:30 NLT

Faith and Prayer

Want your prayers answered? Then believe in what you pray, Jesus essentially told His disciples. Prayer without faith is useless, but real faith will receive responses from God.

> *And all things, whatsoever ye shall ask in prayer, believing, ye shall receive.*
>
> MATTHEW 21:22

> *"If you believe, you will receive whatever you ask for in prayer."*
>
> MATTHEW 21:22 NIV

Jesus' Prayer of Submission

As He faced the supreme crisis of His life on earth, Jesus responded by repeatedly going to His Father in prayer. Clearly the Son did not relish the sacrifice before Him, yet after deep communion, He submitted to His Father's desire.

> *He went away again the second time, and prayed, saying, O my Father, if this cup may not pass away from me, except I drink it, thy will be done.*
>
> MATTHEW 26:42

He went away a second time and prayed,
"My Father, if it is not possible for this cup
to be taken away unless I drink it, may
your will be done."

MATTHEW 26:42 NIV

PRAYER OF THE FORSAKEN

On the cross, Jesus prayed this prayer of desperation, showing that He was able to relate to the emptiness people feel when God seems distant. As the sins of the world weighed Jesus down for that short time, He related to humanity's emptiness without God.

And about the ninth hour Jesus cried
with a loud voice, saying, Eli, Eli,
lama sabachthani? that is to say, My God,
my God, why hast thou forsaken me?

MATTHEW 27:46

About three in the afternoon Jesus cried
out in a loud voice, "Eli, Eli, lema
sabachthani?" (which means "My God,
my God, why have you forsaken me?").

MATTHEW 27:46 NIV

TIME IN PRAYER

Jesus needed time apart to spend with His Father. So He would go off alone to commune with God in heaven. Jesus' example shows believers how important this alone time with God is and how regular it should be.

> *And in the morning, rising up a great while*
> *before day, he went out, and departed into*
> *a solitary place, and there prayed.*
>
> MARK 1:35

> *Very early in the morning, while it was still*
> *dark, Jesus got up, left the house and went*
> *off to a solitary place, where he prayed.*
>
> MARK 1:35 NIV

PRAYER OVERCOMES

"Why," Jesus' disciples asked Him, "couldn't we cast out this spirit that tortured a boy?" The short verse that follows was His answer. Prayer would provide the disciples with the spiritual strength to free people from the sin that wrapped their souls so tightly.

*And he said unto them, This kind can come
forth by nothing, but by prayer and fasting.*

MARK 9:29

*He replied, "This kind can come out only by
prayer."*

MARK 9:29 NIV

PRAYER THAT GLORIFIES GOD

When her cousin Elisabeth recognized that Mary
carried the Savior in her womb, the women rejoiced together. Mary's words in the following
verse have been an encouragement to many believers to trust and celebrate God's work in their lives.

*And Mary said, My soul doth magnify the
Lord, and my spirit hath rejoiced in God
my Saviour.*

LUKE 1:46–47

*And Mary said: "My soul glorifies the Lord
and my spirit rejoices in God my Savior."*

LUKE 1:46–47 NIV

PRAYER AND WISE CHOICES

Before making an important decision, Jesus prayed all night. Though He was God's Son, even He could not live on snippets of prayer here and there. Long, deep prayer was the Master's habit, especially when He faced a duty like choosing His disciples.

> *And it came to pass in those days, that he went out into a mountain to pray, and continued all night in prayer to God. And when it was day, he called unto him his disciples: and of them he chose twelve, whom also he named apostles.*
>
> LUKE 6:12–13

> *One of those days Jesus went out to a mountainside to pray, and spent the night praying to God. When morning came, he called his disciples to him and chose twelve of them, whom he also designated apostles.*
>
> LUKE 6:12–13 NIV

PRAYER FOR ENEMIES

Jesus did not advocate revenge in prayer. Instead, He called His people to forgive and to pray for those who had done them wrong.

*Bless them that curse you, and pray for
them which despitefully use you.*

LUKE 6:28

*"Bless those who curse you. Pray for those
who hurt you."*

LUKE 6:28 NLT

LEARNING TO PRAY

The disciples were keenly aware that Jesus knew much more about prayer than they did. So the students of the great Teacher did the logical thing and asked Him for help. In response, Jesus taught them what we now call the Lord's Prayer.

*And it came to pass, that, as he was praying
in a certain place, when he ceased, one of
his disciples said unto him, Lord, teach us
to pray, as John also taught his disciples.*

LUKE 11:1

*One day Jesus was praying in a certain
place. When he finished, one of his disciples
said to him, "Lord, teach us to pray, just as
John taught his disciples."*

LUKE 11:1 NIV

PERSISTENT PRAYER

Jesus did not allow His disciples to pray with laxity. He could not stand an attitude that said, "I asked God once then gave up." Instead, He wanted them to pray long and hard, trusting that God would respond. Consistent prayer that seeks God's will opens many doors.

And I say unto you, Ask, and it shall be given you; seek, and ye shall find; knock, and it shall be opened unto you. For every one that asketh receiveth; and he that seeketh findeth; and to him that knocketh it shall be opened.

LUKE 11:9–10

"So I say to you: Ask and it will be given to you; seek and you will find; knock and the door will be opened to you. For everyone who asks receives; the one who seeks finds; and to the one who knocks, the door will be opened."

LUKE 11:9–10 NIV

PRAYER ATTITUDE

In Jesus' parable about the tax collector and the Pharisee, two men went to pray in the temple. The Pharisee might have been more important in the eyes of men, and he proudly announced that he was better than the hated tax collector. That "publican," however, had the humble, prayerful attitude that pleased God because he recognized his own wrongdoing.

> *And the publican, standing afar off, would not lift up so much as his eyes unto heaven, but smote upon his breast, saying, God be merciful to me a sinner.*
>
> LUKE 18:13

> *"But the tax collector stood at a distance. He would not even look up to heaven, but beat his breast and said, 'God, have mercy on me, a sinner.'"*
>
> LUKE 18:13 NIV

Unfailing Prayer

Though Peter would fail God for a time, he would not fall away, because Jesus' prayers backed him through the darkest trials of his life. Our Lord has not stopped remembering His people; Romans 8:34 also promises that the Savior will make intercession for all those who believe in Him.

And the Lord said, Simon, Simon, behold, Satan hath desired to have you, that he may sift you as wheat: But I have prayed for thee, that thy faith fail not: and when thou art converted, strengthen thy brethren.

LUKE 22:31–32

"Simon, Simon, Satan has asked to sift each of you like wheat. But I have pleaded in prayer for you, Simon, that your faith should not fail. So when you have repented and turned to me again, strengthen your brothers."

LUKE 22:31–32 NLT

HUMBLE PRAYER

As Jesus faced the cross, the prayer He prayed in the Garden of Gethsemane showed that He had no sinful pride within Him. Obviously, Jesus did not want to end His life on earth by way of crucifixion, yet the Son deferred to the Father's will and plan.

> *Father, if thou be willing, remove this cup from me: nevertheless not my will, but thine, be done.*
>
> LUKE 22:42

> *"Father, if you are willing, take this cup from me; yet not my will, but yours be done."*
>
> LUKE 22:42 NIV

THE MOST FORGIVING PRAYER

Even on the cross, Jesus' gentle spirit sought forgiveness for His enemies. As He suffered to the point of death, He looked to the salvation of those who were harming Him. In doing so, Jesus provided an example of forgiveness for all who trust in Him.

> *Then said Jesus, Father, forgive them; for they know not what they do. And they parted his raiment, and cast lots.*
>
> LUKE 23:34

> *Jesus said, "Father, forgive them, for they do not know what they are doing." And they divided up his clothes by casting lots.*
>
> LUKE 23:34 NIV

SACRIFICE IN PRAYER

Facing the true ultimate sacrifice, Jesus did not think only of Himself. God's glory was uppermost in His mind. Though the task before Him was difficult, Jesus' focus was not on the pain but on God's will.

> *Now is my soul troubled; and what shall I say? Father, save me from this hour: but for this cause came I unto this hour. Father, glorify thy name. Then came there a voice from heaven, saying, I have both glorified it, and will glorify it again.*
>
> JOHN 12:27–28

> *"Now my soul is troubled, and what shall I say? 'Father, save me from this hour'? No, it was for this very reason I came to this hour. Father, glorify your name!" Then a voice came from heaven, "I have glorified it, and will glorify it again."*
>
> JOHN 12:27–28 NIV

PRAYERS OF THE CHOSEN

Because Jesus had chosen the disciples to do His work and bear fruit, their mission would be successful. They had only to ask God for all they needed, and He would answer their prayers.

> *Ye have not chosen me, but I have chosen you, and ordained you, that ye should go and bring forth fruit, and that your fruit should remain: that whatsoever ye shall ask of the Father in my name, he may give it you.*

JOHN 15:16

> *"You did not choose me, but I chose you and appointed you so that you might go and bear fruit—fruit that will last—and so that whatever you ask in my name the Father will give you."*

JOHN 15:16 NIV

SEEING JESUS' GLORY

As He wrapped up His earthly ministry, Jesus prayed that His disciples might know the Father and Himself (John 17:3). As hard days came, Jesus wanted His followers to have a clear picture of the Lord they worshipped. So He asked the Father to give them a sense of His glory. With this, their lives would shine before the world, making their godly mission a success.

Father, I will that they also, whom thou hast given me, be with me where I am; that they may behold my glory, which thou hast given me: for thou lovedst me before the foundation of the world.

JOHN 17:24

"Father, I want those you have given me to be with me where I am, and to see my glory, the glory you have given me because you loved me before the creation of the world."

JOHN 17:24 NIV

DETERMINED PRAYER

After the death, resurrection, and ascension of Jesus, the disciples banded together in prayer, asking God for the needs of their fledgling church. Faithful prayer would become one of the main supports of the faith as the believers faced increasing persecution.

> *These [the disciples] all continued with one accord in prayer and supplication, with the women, and Mary the mother of Jesus, and with his brethren.*
>
> ACTS 1:14

> *They all joined together constantly in prayer, along with the women and Mary the mother of Jesus, and with his brothers.*
>
> ACTS 1:14 NIV

BOLD PRAYING

After being threatened by the temple leaders, John and Peter refused to stop speaking about Jesus. The two apostles returned to their fellow Christians and began to pray, asking not for protection or a change of situation, but for boldness to speak the gospel.

And now, Lord, behold their threatenings:
and grant unto thy servants, that with all
boldness they may speak thy word.

ACTS 4:29

"Now, Lord, consider their threats and
enable your servants to speak your word
with great boldness."

ACTS 4:29 NIV

CONTINUAL PRAYER

Life in the early church was extremely busy for the apostles, so they arranged to select deacons who would deal with some of the physical issues arising in the church. The apostles and teachers had two duties: continual prayer and the ministry of the word. Without prayer, their teaching would never have been as faithful and had the impact it did.

But we will give ourselves continually to
prayer, and to the ministry of the word.

ACTS 6:4

"And [we] will give our attention to prayer
and the ministry of the word."

ACTS 6:4 NIV

PRAYER IN DESPERATE SITUATIONS

Peter had been thrown in prison by King Herod. The news must have shaken the fledgling church, but they knew what to do: they gathered in one place and began to pray. Soon, Peter was knocking at the door, having been released from prison by an angel.

> *He [Peter] came to the house of Mary the mother of John, whose surname was Mark; where many were gathered together praying.*
> ACTS 12:12

> *He [Peter] went to the house of Mary the mother of John, also called Mark, where many people had gathered and were praying.*
> ACTS 12:12 NIV

PRAYER DESPITE AWFUL CIRCUMSTANCES

In Macedonia, Paul and Silas were beaten and thrown in prison for their preaching. How did they respond? They prayed and praised God loudly, trusting in God to resolve their circumstances. Meanwhile, they became a testimony to others in the prison.

And at midnight Paul and Silas prayed,
and sang praises unto God: and the
prisoners heard them.

ACTS 16:25

About midnight Paul and Silas were
praying and singing hymns to God, and the
other prisoners were listening to them.

ACTS 16:25 NIV

PRAYER AT ALL TIMES

In Romans 12 the apostle Paul describes the kind
of Christian life that should be typical of all believers. Prayer is not just for the good times, when
hope is high; it's also important when tribulation
seems the order of the day.

Rejoicing in hope; patient in tribulation;
continuing instant in prayer.

ROMANS 12:12

Rejoice in our confident hope. Be patient in
trouble, and keep on praying.

ROMANS 12:12 NLT

PRAYER FOR OTHERS

Though Paul had never met the Christians in Rome, he knew much about them and longed to visit them. Until that day came, he would pray consistently for them. Paul didn't need to have met the believers in person to be concerned for their spiritual welfare and to devote time and effort to pray for them.

> *For God is my witness, whom I serve with my spirit in the gospel of his Son, that without ceasing I make mention of you always in my prayers; making request, if by any means now at length I might have a prosperous journey by the will of God to come unto you.*

ROMANS 1:9–10

> *God, whom I serve in my spirit in preaching the gospel of his Son, is my witness how constantly I remember you in my prayers at all times; and I pray that now at last by God's will the way may be opened for me to come to you.*

ROMANS 1:9–10 NIV

PRAYER IN WEAKNESS

Because he did not always feel strong, the apostle Paul knew how much help his Lord could be in prayer. Even when Paul could not find the words, he knew God's Spirit was struggling for him in prayer. The Spirit brings our needs before the Father on a deep, wordless level.

Likewise the Spirit also helpeth our infirmities: for we know not what we should pray for as we ought: but the Spirit itself maketh intercession for us with groanings which cannot be uttered. And he that searcheth the hearts knoweth what is the mind of the Spirit, because he maketh intercession for the saints according to the will of God.

ROMANS 8:26–27

In the same way, the Spirit helps us in our weakness. We do not know what we ought to pray for, but the Spirit himself intercedes for us through wordless groans. And he who searches our hearts knows the mind of the Spirit, because the Spirit intercedes for God's people in accordance with the will of God.

ROMANS 8:26–27 NIV

Prayer and Tongues

Though Paul did not forbid speaking in tongues, he wanted everyone in the church to understand what was said. If a message was given in an unknown language, the apostle encouraged the Corinthians to pray to be able interpret what was spoken. Both spirit and mind could then be engaged together.

Wherefore let him that speaketh in an unknown tongue pray that he may interpret. For if I pray in an unknown tongue, my spirit prayeth, but my understanding is unfruitful. What is it then? I will pray with the spirit, and I will pray with the understanding also.

1 Corinthians 14:13–15

For this reason the one who speaks in a tongue should pray that they may interpret what they say. For if I pray in a tongue, my spirit prays, but my mind is unfruitful. So what shall I do? I will pray with my spirit, but I will also pray with my understanding.

1 Corinthians 14:13–15 NIV

Prayer for Another's Ministry

While Paul set about his often-dangerous ministry, the Corinthians and others in the New Testament church took part in his mission by praying. The apostle appreciated their help. While Paul trusted that God would deliver him from troubles, he also knew the importance of having believers praying consistently for him.

[God] delivered us from so great a death, and doth deliver: in whom we trust that he will yet deliver us; ye also helping together by prayer for us, that for the gift bestowed upon us by the means of many persons thanks may be given by many on our behalf.

2 Corinthians 1:10–11

He has delivered us from such a deadly peril, and he will deliver us again. On him we have set our hope that he will continue to deliver us, as you help us by your prayers. Then many will give thanks on our behalf for the gracious favor granted us in answer to the prayers of many.

2 Corinthians 1:10–11 NIV

A PRAYER ANSWERED WITH NO

Three times the apostle Paul asked God to remove a problem he called "a thorn in the flesh." But God answered no. The apostle concluded that the physical trial was designed to keep him from falling victim to pride (see 2 Corinthians 12:7). He accepted God's decision not to heal him.

For this thing I besought the Lord thrice, that it might depart from me. And he said unto me, My grace is sufficient for thee: for my strength is made perfect in weakness. Most gladly therefore will I rather glory in my infirmities, that the power of Christ may rest upon me.

2 CORINTHIANS 12:8–9

Three times I pleaded with the Lord to take it away from me. But he said to me, "My grace is sufficient for you, for my power is made perfect in weakness." Therefore I will boast all the more gladly about my weaknesses, so that Christ's power may rest on me.

2 CORINTHIANS 12:8–9 NIV

A PRAYER BLESSING

Though this might more properly be called a blessing, what church members would not be glad to have a leader pray for them this way? The apostle Paul must certainly have prayed for the Galatians, who were caught up in doctrinal confusion.

Grace be to you and peace from God the Father, and from our Lord Jesus Christ, who gave himself for our sins, that he might deliver us from this present evil world, according to the will of God and our Father: to whom be glory for ever and ever. Amen.

GALATIANS 1:3–5

Grace and peace to you from God our Father and the Lord Jesus Christ, who gave himself for our sins to rescue us from the present evil age, according to the will of our God and Father, to whom be glory for ever and ever. Amen.

GALATIANS 1:3–5 NIV

Prayer of Thanksgiving

As soon as Paul knew about the Ephesians' faith in Jesus, he began to give thanks to the Lord for it. But a one-time prayer was not enough for the apostle. He continued to pray for these people as beloved brothers and sisters in Christ.

After I heard of your faith in the Lord Jesus, and love unto all the saints, [I did] cease not to give thanks for you, making mention of you in my prayers.

EPHESIANS 1:15–16

Ever since I heard about your faith in the Lord Jesus and your love for all God's people, I have not stopped giving thanks for you, remembering you in my prayers.

EPHESIANS 1:15–16 NIV

GIVING THANKS IN PRAYER

The apostle Paul encouraged the Ephesians not to forget praise and thanks in their prayer life. Whether God has given us a great singing voice or not, He loves it when we honor Him with various kinds of songs.

> *Speaking to yourselves in psalms and hymns and spiritual songs, singing and making melody in your heart to the Lord; giving thanks always for all things unto God and the Father in the name of our Lord Jesus Christ.*
>
> EPHESIANS 5:19–20

> *Speaking to one another with psalms, hymns, and songs from the Spirit. Sing and make music from your heart to the Lord, always giving thanks to God the Father for everything, in the name of our Lord Jesus Christ.*
>
> EPHESIANS 5:19–20 NIV

PRAYING BROADLY

As we saw earlier, the apostle Paul told Christians to "pray without ceasing" (1 Thessalonians 5:17). In Ephesians 6, he encourages "all kinds of prayers and requests" (verse 18 NIV). When we pray in God's Spirit—that is, humbly allowing Him to align our wishes with the Father's—there are no restrictions on our prayers. We can praise God, ask Him for help, request the salvation of others, confess sin. . .anything that is important to us and our world is fair game.

Praying always with all prayer and supplication in the Spirit.

EPHESIANS 6:18

Pray in the Spirit on all occasions with all kinds of prayers and requests.

EPHESIANS 6:18 NIV

Prayer for Love and Knowledge

While we rarely forget to pray for physical needs—health, finances, and the like—the apostle Paul's prayer for the Christians in Philippi reminds us we should also pray for spiritual needs. Believers, who are called to love God and their fellow man (Matthew 22:36–40), can grow their love through knowledge and discernment, which comes from scripture. God is happy to answer a prayer like this one that Paul lifted up for the Philippian Christians.

And this I pray, that your love may abound yet more and more in knowledge and in all judgment; that ye may approve things that are excellent; that ye may be sincere and without offence till the day of Christ.

PHILIPPIANS 1:9–10

And this is my prayer: that your love may abound more and more in knowledge and depth of insight, so that you may be able to discern what is best and may be pure and blameless for the day of Christ.

PHILIPPIANS 1:9–10 NIV

CALMING PRAYER

Don't worry, be prayerful, Paul told the Christians of Philippi. Instead of thinking the worst, pray—and give God, who is always faithful, thanks for what He has done.

> *Be careful for nothing; but in every thing by*
> *prayer and supplication with thanksgiving*
> *let your requests be made known unto God.*
> PHILIPPIANS 4:6

> *Don't worry about anything; instead, pray*
> *about everything. Tell God what you need,*
> *and thank him for all he has done.*
> PHILIPPIANS 4:6 NLT

DEVOTED TO PRAYER

Paul's prescription for dealing with heresy? A better understanding of doctrine, along with prayer. After the apostle had clarified doctrinal issues, he asked the Colossians to pray devotedly, including him in their prayers as he took the gospel message to the world.

Continue in prayer, and watch in the same with thanksgiving; withal praying also for us, that God would open unto us a door of utterance, to speak the mystery of Christ, for which I am also in bonds.

COLOSSIANS 4:2–3

Devote yourselves to prayer, being watchful and thankful. And pray for us, too, that God may open a door for our message, so that we may proclaim the mystery of Christ, for which I am in chains.

COLOSSIANS 4:2–3 NIV

PRAYER FOR BELIEVERS

Paul gave thanks for the Thessalonians, who brought him joy in his ministry. In some places, spreading the gospel was a hard task, so he was always thankful for those who had accepted the message and grew in love for Christ. Paul's example of thankfulness can inspire any believer to remember the good things God has done, and then praise Him for them.

For what thanks can we render to God again for you, for all the joy wherewith we joy for your sakes before our God; night and day praying exceedingly that we might see your face, and might perfect that which is lacking in your faith?

1 THESSALONIANS 3:9–10

How can we thank God enough for you in return for all the joy we have in the presence of our God because of you? Night and day we pray most earnestly that we may see you again and supply what is lacking in your faith.

1 THESSALONIANS 3:9–10 NIV

Ceaseless, Thankful Prayer

According to Paul's first letter to the Thessalonians, Christians should never stop praying. And in these continual prayers, they should give thanks, whatever their circumstances.

> *Pray without ceasing. In every thing give thanks: for this is the will of God in Christ Jesus concerning you.*
> 1 THESSALONIANS 5:17–18

> *Pray continually, give thanks in all circumstances; for this is God's will for you in Christ Jesus.*
> 1 THESSALONIANS 5:17–18 NIV

PRAYER FOR THE PASTOR

Paul, who until this point had been praying for the Thessalonian church, now asked them to pray for him and his ministry. Today's church pastors would be blessed by such prayers from their congregations.

> *Finally, brethren, pray for us, that the word*
> *of the Lord may have free course, and be*
> *glorified, even as it is with you.*
>
> 2 THESSALONIANS 3:1

> *As for other matters, brothers and sisters,*
> *pray for us that the message of the Lord may*
> *spread rapidly and be honored, just as it*
> *was with you.*
>
> 2 THESSALONIANS 3:1 NIV

A Purpose for Prayer

Paul exhorted his young protégé Timothy to encourage the people under his ministry to pray for those in authority. This instruction applied even though Roman leaders often mistreated Christians. Prayer could lead to peace for the believers.

I exhort therefore, that, first of all, supplications, prayers, intercessions, and giving of thanks, be made for all men; for kings, and for all that are in authority; that we may lead a quiet and peaceable life in all godliness and honesty.

1 Timothy 2:1–2

I urge, then, first of all, that petitions, prayers, intercession and thanksgiving be made for all people—for kings and all those in authority, that we may live peaceful and quiet lives in all godliness and holiness.

1 Timothy 2:1–2 NIV

PRAYER FOR FAITHFUL FRIENDS

Onesiphorus and his family had been faithful supporters of Paul's ministry while he was in chains for the faith, a time when many were disloyal to the apostle. This man and his family are mentioned only twice in scripture; some speculate that Onesiphorus had died, since Paul speaks of him in the past tense and mentions his "household" in a blessing given early in 2 Timothy.

The Lord give mercy unto the house of Onesiphorus; for he oft refreshed me, and was not ashamed of my chain: but, when he was in Rome, he sought me out very diligently, and found me. The Lord grant unto him that he may find mercy of the Lord in that day: and in how many things he ministered unto me at Ephesus, thou knowest very well.

2 TIMOTHY 1:16–18

May the Lord show mercy to the household of Onesiphorus, because he often refreshed me and was not ashamed of my chains. On the contrary, when he was in Rome, he searched hard for me until he found me. May the Lord grant that he will find mercy

from the Lord on that day! You know very
well in how many ways he helped me in
Ephesus.

2 TIMOTHY 1:16–18 NIV

GRACE FOR A DIFFICULT MINISTRY

The apostle Paul prayed for "grace and peace" on
Titus's difficult ministry. The young leader was
to appoint elders in the church and rebuke those
who were spreading false teaching. What a blessing it must have been for Titus to know that Paul
had confidence in him—and that his mentor was
lifting him and his work up before the Lord.

Grace, mercy, and peace, from God the
Father and the Lord Jesus Christ our Saviour.

TITUS 1:4

Grace and peace from God the Father and
Christ Jesus our Savior.

TITUS 1:4 NIV

PRAYER FOR A FELLOW CHRISTIAN

It was unlikely that Philemon jumped for joy over this letter from Paul. The apostle wanted the slave owner to forgive a runaway slave whom Paul had led to Christ. In this very tactful epistle, Paul smoothed the way by telling Philemon that he prayed for him—and reminded him of their partnership in faith.

I thank my God, making mention of thee always in my prayers. . . . That the communication of thy faith may become effectual by the acknowledging of every good thing which is in you in Christ Jesus.

PHILEMON 4, 6

I always thank my God as I remember you in my prayers. . . . I pray that your partnership with us in the faith may be effective in deepening your understanding of every good thing we share for the sake of Christ.

PHILEMON 4, 6 NIV

BOLD PRAYING

The writer of Hebrews, who does not name himself in the letter, tells us not to be shy about bringing our needs before God. He knows what we lack, and He wants to help us. When we need mercy and grace, God is waiting with each—just waiting for us to ask.

> *Let us therefore come boldly unto the throne of grace, that we may obtain mercy, and find grace to help in time of need.*
>
> HEBREWS 4:16

> *Let us then approach God's throne of grace with confidence, so that we may receive mercy and find grace to help us in our time of need.*
>
> HEBREWS 4:16 NIV

Prayer for Wisdom

James, believed by many to be the half brother of Jesus, encouraged Christians to pray for wisdom —and to pray fearlessly. Wavering in prayer shows a lack of faith, and the one who doubts should eradicate that before praying. To pray in faith means trusting in the goodness and power of God, who wants us to share His wisdom so we can make good decisions.

> *If any of you lack wisdom, let him ask of God, that giveth to all men liberally, and upbraideth not; and it shall be given him. But let him ask in faith, nothing wavering. For he that wavereth is like a wave of the sea driven with the wind and tossed. For let not that man think that he shall receive any thing of the Lord.*
>
> JAMES 1:5–7

> *If any of you lacks wisdom, you should ask God, who gives generously to all without finding fault, and it will be given to you. But when you ask, you must believe and not doubt, because the one who doubts is like a wave of the sea, blown and tossed by the wind. That person should not expect to receive anything from the Lord.*
>
> JAMES 1:5–7 NIV

Unanswered Prayer

James gives a quick answer to Christians who complain that God does not answer their prayers. Look at your intentions, he more or less tells them. If you are seeking your own will instead of God's, don't be surprised when He doesn't give you what you want. Only hearts that look to obey God can be powerful in prayer. Of course, not every unanswered prayer is selfish. . .but perhaps God has another plan and is working out something better in our lives.

> *Ye ask, and receive not, because ye ask amiss, that ye may consume it upon your lusts.*
>
> JAMES 4:3

> *When you ask, you do not receive, because you ask with wrong motives, that you may spend what you get on your pleasures.*
>
> JAMES 4:3 NIV

PRAISING GOD

Early in his first letter, Peter sets the tone by praising God for the hope believers have in Jesus Christ, who died and rose again so they could gain eternal life. Though the Christians he wrote to were suffering persecution, they should still praise God, remembering the blessings He provided.

Blessed be the God and Father of our Lord Jesus Christ, which according to his abundant mercy hath begotten us again unto a lively hope by the resurrection of Jesus Christ from the dead.

1 PETER 1:3

All praise to God, the Father of our Lord Jesus Christ. It is by his great mercy that we have been born again, because God raised Jesus Christ from the dead. Now we live with great expectation.

1 PETER 1:3 NLT

BLESSINGS OF GOD

Despite the troubles the believers had faced and the false teachers who troubled them, Peter reminded the recipients of his letter to seek the blessings of God's grace and peace. They could do this by knowing Him deeply, turning to the Lord Jesus for knowledge in times of need. This would then be an occasion for praise.

> *Grace and peace be multiplied unto you through the knowledge of God, and of Jesus our Lord.*
>
> 2 PETER 1:2

> *Grace and peace be yours in abundance through the knowledge of God and of Jesus our Lord.*
>
> 2 PETER 1:2 NIV

OVERCOMING SIN

Who can doubt that those who seek to overcome sin confess their sins to God? Though 1 John does not mention prayer specifically, the truths of prayer are throughout its pages. And those who abide in God have a relationship with Him in prayer.

> *Whosoever abideth in him sinneth not: whosoever sinneth hath not seen him, neither known him.*
>
> 1 JOHN 3:6

> *No one who lives in him keeps on sinning. No one who continues to sin has either seen him or known him.*
>
> 1 JOHN 3:6 NIV

CONFIDENCE IN PRAYER

Those who know God need not feel guilty for sins God has forgiven, and they can ask in prayer, knowing that He will answer. Belonging to God means believers have set their ways in obedience to Him and are guided by Him. So God hears their prayers and answers.

> *Beloved, if our heart condemn us not, then have we confidence toward God. And what-soever we ask, we receive of him, because*

*we keep his commandments, and do those
things that are pleasing in his sight.*

1 JOHN 3:21–22

*Dear friends, if our hearts do not condemn
us, we have confidence before God and
receive from him anything we ask,
because we keep his commands and do
what pleases him.*

1 JOHN 3:21–22 NIV

PRAYER IN TROUBLE AND JOY

James 5:13–18 describes many ways prayer is
necessary for Christians. But whether they're in
affliction or joy, believers should turn to prayer
and praise. There's never a reason to give up on
prayer, no matter how dire the situation, and no
one should ignore praise when life is happy.

*Is any among you afflicted? let him pray. Is
any merry? let him sing psalms.*

JAMES 5:13

*Are any of you suffering hardships? You
should pray. Are any of you happy? You
should sing praises.*

JAMES 5:13 NLT

INVOCATION OF BLESSING

John invokes a blessing of grace, mercy, and peace on the "elect lady" in this brief, intimate letter. As we think of others in our prayers, do we ask God for blessings to be showered down on them? Even when we don't know what would be best for our friends, we know that God's grace, mercy, and peace will always fit the bill.

Grace be with you, mercy, and peace, from God the Father, and from the Lord Jesus Christ, the Son of the Father, in truth and love.

2 JOHN 3

Grace, mercy and peace from God the Father and from Jesus Christ, the Father's Son, will be with us in truth and love.

2 JOHN 3 NIV

PRAYER FOR BLESSING

John had heard of Gaius's effective Christian walk. In this letter of praise and encouragement, John asks God for the physical blessings of prosperity and health to be added to the prosperity of Gaius's soul. No one need fear to ask for physical and spiritual prosperity for another believer.

> *Beloved, I wish above all things that thou mayest prosper and be in health, even as thy soul prospereth.*
>
> 3 JOHN 2

> *Dear friend, I pray that you may enjoy good health and that all may go well with you, even as your soul is getting along well.*
>
> 3 JOHN 2 NIV

PRAYING IN THE SPIRIT

As Christians faced false teachers, Jude encouraged them to hang tough. He reminded them of prophecies that such teachers would come, and then he gave them advice on their response: stay faithful and pray. This, Jude said, would keep the believers strong in their faith.

But ye, beloved, building up yourselves on your most holy faith, praying in the Holy Ghost, keep yourselves in the love of God, looking for the mercy of our Lord Jesus Christ unto eternal life.

JUDE 20–21

But you, dear friends, by building yourselves up in your most holy faith and praying in the Holy Spirit, keep yourselves in God's love as you wait for the mercy of our Lord Jesus Christ to bring you to eternal life.

JUDE 20–21 NIV

SONG OF PRAISE

The book of Revelation gives us a sneak peek at the worship of the future: praises sung to the Lamb of God, Jesus. When we consider the redemption He has bought us, shouldn't we join in the singing?

And they sung a new song, saying, Thou art worthy to take the book, and to open the seals thereof: for thou wast slain, and hast redeemed us to God by thy blood out of every kindred, and tongue, and people, and nation.

REVELATION 5:9

And they sang a new song with these words: "You are worthy to take the scroll and break its seals and open it. For you were slaughtered, and your blood has ransomed people for God from every tribe and language and people and nation."

REVELATION 5:9 NLT

PRAISE THAT GLORIFIES GOD'S VICTORY

In the end times, following seven plagues of judgment that God pours on the wicked earth, His faithful people respond with praise for His victory. This is a true prayer of praise that wells from the hearts of God's own.

Great and marvellous are thy works, Lord God Almighty; just and true are thy ways, thou King of saints. Who shall not fear thee, O Lord, and glorify thy name? for thou only art holy: for all nations shall come and worship before thee; for thy judgments are made manifest.

REVELATION 15:3–4

"Great and marvelous are your deeds, Lord God Almighty. Just and true are your ways, King of the nations. Who will not fear you, Lord, and bring glory to your name? For you alone are holy. All nations will come and worship before you, for your righteous acts have been revealed."

REVELATION 15:3–4 NIV

5. JESUS' TEACHING ON PRAYER

Who would know more about speaking to God the Father than His own Son? It's not unreasonable to expect that Jesus, above all others, would be able to teach His people to pray, and He does exactly that, showing Christians how to prayerfully connect with God.

The Gospels provide us with Jesus' teaching that shows us both how and how *not* to pray. The Son's inside understanding of communication with the Father gives us direction in our praying and an understanding of prayer that appears nowhere else in scripture.

For Jesus, prayer was not a drudgery to be completed each morning, but a joyful method of communication with the Father. Asking and receiving, He told His disciples, would make their joy full (John 16:24). That assumes that we will not only ask God for help, but that we will receive it too.

The Gospel of Matthew includes the greatest number of references to prayer. It seems obvious that Matthew's past affected his perspective on prayer and the way he recorded Jesus' words on the subject. Matthew's account has much to do with human frailty in prayer and God's greatness as He responds to our communication with Him.

SETTLING GRUDGES FIRST

The former tax collector began by recounting Jesus' teaching that a believer who knows someone else is holding a grudge against them should first try to make things right with the other person (Matthew 5:23–24). Later, Matthew reported Jesus' command to love and pray for enemies (verses 44–45). No doubt his own less-than-perfect past as a tax collector made Matthew keenly aware of his own failings, so Jesus' words stuck with him and found a place in his accounting of the life of his Lord.

Matthew makes it clear that for Jesus, prayer was not simply made up of words—it also required right action that put those words into the lives of people.

WHAT PRAYER ISN'T—AND IS

Before Jesus gave the disciples the Lord's Prayer—His most famous direction on what prayer should be—He offered warnings about what prayer was *not* meant to be:

> *"And when you pray, you shall not be like the hypocrites. For they love to pray standing in*

*the synagogues and on the corners of
the streets, that they may be seen by men.
Assuredly, I say to you, they have their
reward. But you, when you pray, go into
your room, and when you have shut your
door, pray to your Father who is in the
secret place; and your Father who sees in
secret will reward you openly. And when
you pray, do not use vain repetitions as the
heathen do. For they think that they will be
heard for their many words."*

MATTHEW 6:5–7 NKJV

The disciples had seen Pharisees standing in public, loudly proclaiming what they thought were holy prayers. But Jesus remained unimpressed with their pseudoreligious words. They had no more value to Him than the loud, self-seeking, and ungodly heathen prayers of people from other nations.

Religion was not important to Jesus; faith was. So personal prayer is a God-man connection that should be done with a humble heart, never for show. Those who seek commendation for such public prayers, Jesus told His disciples, have gotten all they can expect—and all the notice and affirmation comes from humans, not the Lord. Praying to get the attention of others is not really prayer, but pride. It was true in the disciples' day, and it is no less true in our own lives.

Mark 7 and Matthew 15 recount another of Jesus' reactions to the Pharisees, who the Lord said, referring to a prophecy of Isaiah, "These people draw near to Me with their mouth, and honor Me with their lips, but their heart is far from Me" (Matthew 15:8 NKJV). The self-righteous religious critics had complained that Jesus' disciples did not wash their hands before eating, a pharisaical tradition they held in high esteem. But this gave Jesus an opportunity to contrast their keeping of mostly man-made laws with the hard-heartedness that so often characterized their thinking:

> *"All too well you reject the commandment of God, that you may keep your tradition. For Moses said, 'Honor your father and your mother'; and, 'He who curses father or mother, let him be put to death.' But you say, 'If a man says to his father or mother, "Whatever profit you might have received from me is Corban"—' (that is, a gift to God), then you no longer let him do anything for his father or his mother."*

> MARK 7:9–12 NKJV

By obeying their law of false holiness, the Pharisees ignored the law of God to honor parents (Exodus 20:12).

Jesus knew hypocrites when He saw them—and He pointed out that what you pray doesn't mean much if your heart is not pure. Those who don't love God don't get far with their prayers, because they put people's commandments, like washing before eating, ahead of God's. Self-serving prayers mean nothing to the Lord, and He wants no gifts that break His laws of kindness and charity. While Jesus Himself kept the law perfectly, He also kept the spirit of the law, reflecting God's love for His people. That's what He expects of Christians today.

Luke dealt with the same Pharisaical attitude when he recorded the parable of the Pharisee and the tax collector (18:9–14). Though tax collectors were known to take extra money from those who could ill afford it, the one in Jesus' parable was the man God commended. Why? Because he went to God in humble prayer, confessing and turning from wrongdoing. Meanwhile, the self-righteous Pharisee praised his own supposed goodness. Clueless as to his own sin, he remained spiritually lost.

Real prayer focuses on truth (John 4:23–24)—and the truth is that, though we are God's people, we often fail. Nothing is hidden from Him, and He knows what we need even better than (and before) we do. Since Jesus experienced the pressures and temptations of human life, He sympathizes with us, and we can go before Him confidently (Hebrews 4:16). There is no need to hide behind a mask.

And we need not pray what we might think God wants to hear. We can go to Him openly, without fear, trusting that He already has plans to help us (Hebrews 13:6).

THE LORD'S PRAYER

The Bible's best-known prayer is doubtless the Lord's Prayer, which appears in both Matthew 6:9–13 and Luke 11:2–4. When the disciples asked Him how to pray, Jesus responded with this (Luke 11:1). But it is not so much a prayer to be repeated as it is a template combining praise and worship, and teaching us to seek God's will in our lives, ask for our daily needs, and offer both confession and willing obedience to the Lord.

Notice that Jesus told the disciples to pray "after this manner" (Matthew 6:9), not "with these words." As a template, the Lord's Prayer is not a rigid rule, but a guideline for the most balanced prayers. When we attempt to include all of its elements in our prayers, we are less likely to over-emphasize one aspect of prayer to the detriment of others.

> *After this manner therefore pray ye: Our Father which art in heaven, hallowed be thy name. Thy kingdom come, thy will be done in earth, as it is in heaven. Give us this day our daily bread. And forgive us our debts, as we forgive our debtors. And lead us not into temptation, but deliver us from evil: for thine is the kingdom, and the power, and the glory, for ever. Amen.*
> MATTHEW 6:9–13

Our prayers are directed to the Father in heaven, the One whose "name," indicating all that He is, is "hallowed." In other words, God's nature is holy. According to Jesus' example prayer, we should come to Him with reverence, acknowledging how great He is—how totally beyond ourselves.

When our prayers look to God's coming kingdom, we acknowledge that this world is not all we can expect. There is a kingdom to come in which God will rule without human sin interfering. Until that time, we ask that His will should be done on earth as it is done in heaven. By trying to do God's will in the here and now, Christians hope to have a positive impact on the world, bringing heaven down to earth as much as possible.

"Give us this day our daily bread" means we ask God for our needs day by day. We cannot hoard worldly goods in a heavenly way; instead we ask His provision through the day we have before us. Naturally we have more needs than simply bread; they all can be brought before God each day.

The Lord's Prayer highlights another need—that of forgiveness, since we fall short of God's perfection daily. As we ask God's forgiveness for our own sins, Jesus reminds us to offer forgiveness to those who have wronged us too. Without that, He will not freely forgive our sins.

Though Luke leaves it out, Matthew 6:13 includes the worshipful ending, "And lead us not into temptation, but deliver us from evil: for thine is the kingdom, and the power, and the glory, for ever. Amen." When God is in control of our lives, we can avoid temptations and see His kingdom worked out through us.

At times our prayers may focus more on praise and less on our needs, or vice versa. But throughout our lives we want to find the balance of including all the elements of the Lord's prayer in our own praying. When we feel our communion with God is out of whack, we can easily look at the Lord's Prayer to see where we've gone wrong. Fine-tuning our prayers according to this model will help us rediscover our closeness with God.

THE POWER OF PRAYER

The Lord's Prayer was not Jesus' only teaching on the subject. The Gospel writers record a number of other truths Jesus imparted to them.

Matthew reported these words of Jesus: "Ask, and it shall be given you; seek, and ye shall find; knock, and it shall be opened unto you: for every one that asketh receiveth; and he that seeketh findeth; and to him that knocketh it shall be opened" (Matthew 7:7–8). The former tax collector, who had been forgiven much, appreciated that God had not cut him off but rather brought him into many blessings. And in verses 9–11 Matthew captured Jesus' comparison of God to a good father, who only provides good things to his praying children.

Matthew also highlighted the power of a faithful community, even a tiny one, in prayer. He was the only Gospel writer to record Jesus' teaching, "Again I say to you that if two of you agree on earth concerning anything that they ask, it will be done for them by My Father in heaven. For where two or three are gathered together in My name, I am there in the midst of them" (Matthew 18:19–20 NKJV).

The author of the second Gospel, Mark, shared Jesus' teaching that faith—not numbers or anything else—is the power behind prayer: "Therefore I say to you, whatever things you ask when you pray, believe that you receive them, and you will have them" (Mark 11:24 NKJV). Such faith, Jesus had said in the previous verse, could move mountains.

In the Garden of Gethsemane, as Jesus faced His sacrificial death on the cross, He was concerned that His followers took prayer so lightly. After going off by Himself to pray, Jesus returned to find the disciples sleeping. "Simon, are you sleeping?" He asked. "Could you not watch one hour? Watch and pray, lest you enter into temptation. The spirit indeed is willing, but the flesh is weak" (Mark 14:37–38 NKJV). It would have been to Peter's benefit to have spent that time in prayer, as he would soon discover.

But prayer's effectiveness is not limited by the difficult situations of this world. Following His list of blessings called the Beatitudes, Jesus highlighted the importance of prayer when life is unpleasant: "Bless those who curse you, and pray for those who spitefully use you" (Luke 6:28 NKJV). When others hurt us, we rarely feel like praying for them—but our Lord calls us to do so. Responding in kind is of little use, but responding in faith, with God's brand of forgiveness, can change lives.

"Don't stop asking God" might be the catchphrase for Jesus' next teaching in the Gospel of Luke, which encourages persistent prayer. The Lord let us know that God will always respond with whatever is best for us:

> *"So I say to you, ask, and it will be given to you; seek, and you will find; knock, and it will be opened to you. For everyone who asks receives, and he who seeks finds, and to him who knocks it will be opened. If a son asks for bread from any father among you, will he give him a stone? Or if he asks for a fish, will he give him a serpent instead of a fish? Or if he asks for an egg, will he offer him a scorpion? If you then, being evil, know how to give good gifts to your children, how much more will your heavenly Father give the Holy Spirit to those who ask Him!"*

LUKE 11:9–13 NKJV

Several chapters later, Luke provided a picture of persistence in prayer with Jesus' parable of the widow who would not give up trying to change a judge's mind (Luke 18:1–8). Unlike the judge in this story, God does not need us to pester Him, though He sometimes has His own reasons for delaying an answer. But as we pray with the belief that God knows our lives and needs, our prayers often change to become more in line with His will.

Prayer is not something to be taken lightly. James 5:16 promises, "The effectual fervent prayer of a righteous man availeth much." When it becomes a regular part of our lives, prayer can become a blessing to us and those around us.

6. JESUS' EXAMPLE OF PRAYER

While Matthew records much of Jesus' *teaching* on prayer, Luke is the writer who focuses most on His *example* in prayer. Through the detailed reporting of the third Gospel, we see how often Jesus went apart for prayer or taught His disciples about the subject.

Early in His ministry, Jesus started off praying in public: "When all the people were baptized, it came to pass that Jesus also was baptized; and while He prayed, the heaven was opened" (Luke 3:21 NKJV). We don't know what He said, but it was a prayer God immediately responded to. Like a dove, the Holy Spirit came upon Jesus, and God the Father made it publicly known that this was His Son. What a wonderful beginning to a ministry!

Still, much of Jesus' prayer time was spent in private, according to Luke 5:16 (NKJV): "He Himself often withdrew into the wilderness and prayed." Jesus often removed Himself from the sight of others to commune with God, rather than drawing attention to Himself as the Pharisees did with their loud but empty prayers. What Jesus shared with the Father was intensely personal. As He built His ministry and faced increasing challenges, there would be even more need for private prayer.

Jesus' success did not depend on the attention and appreciation of others. From the Father, He took His direction and gained His strength, so prayer was a regular habit—especially before serious events such as the choosing of His apostles (Luke 6:12–16) or the discussion of His being the Messiah (9:18). And it was during prayer that the apostles saw Jesus transfigured and meeting with Moses and Elijah (9:28–36). After feeding the five thousand, He went apart to pray in solitude then went to the disciples, walking on water (Matthew 14:22–27).

Prayer and the Savior's wonderful works were closely connected.

PRAYERS KNOWN AND UNKNOWN

In Jesus' recorded prayers, such the Lord's Prayer or the one in the Garden of Gethsemane, He always focused on the Father's will. But many of Jesus' prayers are unknown to us. Though the Gospel writers show Him spending time with the heavenly Father, they recorded no words.

Still, from the details we do have, we can be sure Jesus was the ultimate prayer warrior.

Like us, Jesus had questions and doubts that He brought to the Father. Before He began to pray in Gethsemane, He told His disciples, "My soul is overwhelmed with sorrow to the point of death" (Matthew 26:38 NIV). In His humanity, Jesus struggled to do God's will and accept the cross, even to the point of asking the Father to remove "this cup" from Him (verse 39). But in the same verse, Jesus bowed to His Father's will and agreed to go to the cross. Prayer, for Jesus, was not necessarily getting what He wanted, but doing what His Father desired.

This prayer was recorded for our encouragement. When we wonder why our prayers seem so hard, we can know that God has not deserted us—any more than He left Jesus in His hardest moments.

Jesus prayed the same prayer three times in Gethsemane, and returned to find His disciples sleeping each time. We should never expect prayer to be simple or the solution to our problems quick. What was difficult for the Son of God will probably not be easy for us either. But we are privileged to follow Jesus' example of faithful, obedient prayer.

In John 17, after telling the disciples that He would soon leave them, Jesus briefly prayed for

Himself, asking the Father to glorify Him and help Him fulfill His purpose for coming to earth. Then Jesus prayed a longer, tender prayer for the men who would carry His good news to the world, asking the Father to support and protect them in their mission. What an encouragement this must have been to the disciples, pained to think that Jesus would no longer be physically by their side.

But Jesus went even further in His prayer, asking the Father to bless all those who would believe in Him, down through the centuries (John 17:20–26), even those of us who follow Him today. The gospel mission did not end with Jesus' death or resurrection or ascension. It will not be done until His return to earth to reclaim all His saints.

On the cross, in His final and most public prayer, Jesus asked forgiveness for those who were killing Him: "Father, forgive them, for they do not know what they do" (Luke 23:34 NKJV). What comfort that offers us, when we inadvertently fail: we know that our Savior understands and has compassion on us and is willing to forgive our sins.

HOW DID JESUS PRAY?

From the examples we have, we can tell that our Savior's prayers were very intimate. The relationship He has with His Father is one of trust and confidence. So His prayers on earth were a deep communication of relationship, not laundry lists of things He wanted the Father to do for Him. He and His Father were working in tandem to accomplish Jesus' mission on earth, yet there was never any doubt as to who was in charge. Jesus never tried to manipulate His Father, as we sometimes do. Though He struggled to face the cross and would have preferred another option, He went through with God the Father's will.

We may read Jesus' prayers and wish we could speak to God that way, with the confidence that He will respond and the surety that He will help. Jesus, of course, was and is perfect, and we are not—though His perfection has been attributed to us by God's grace. So we confidently do what He tells us, to "ask and it shall be given you; seek, and ye shall find; knock, and it shall be opened unto you" (Matthew 7:7). Our self-doubt should not keep us from prayer, because God is eager to provide for our needs. Though we may not always get what we expect, we can trust that just as Jesus was blessed by the Father, we will be too.

Our confidence need not be in our own ability to pray well, but in the God who grants our requests or defers them in His own perfect will. Like the Lord Jesus, when we live in a love relationship with the Father, we'll focus on honesty and forthrightness with Him. God's choices in answering our prayers may still remain mysterious, but we can trust that He will never leave us in the lurch.

7. PRAYING THE SCRIPTURES

Where do we turn when we need to know how to pray in ways that please God? Though many Christians seem to think prayer should be an easy, natural thing, there are times when it is anything but. When we've made the same request of God over and over, and the answer does not come, do we fall into resentment and stop praying? Or do we do as Jesus advised us in Matthew 7:7 and persist? How do we even know if we are praying in ways that please God?

Scripture provides ample ideas for prayer—for our own need to draw closer to God, for knowing His will, for the salvation of others, and for physical needs. And if we have gotten off course and need to fine-tune our requests to be more in line with His will, God's Word can also redirect our praying.

SCRIPTURE'S IMPORTANCE IN PRAYER

When our prayer lives are less than exciting, scripture is a wonderful place to begin. From its pages, we learn what God expects of us, how we can relate with others, and when we have fallen out of His will and need to repent. But scripture also shows us ways to praise God for His goodness, whether our lives are hard or going well.

Often, as we read the Bible, we find examples that relate directly to our lives. When we read a praise that seems appropriate in our lives too, do we offer it up to God?

When the Jewish religious leaders told Peter and John that they could not preach Christ, the two apostles refused to obey men instead of God. Though the leaders threatened Peter and John, they also feared the crowds that were glorifying God because of the apostles' miraculous healing of a lame man. Peter and John went free—God had provided a way out for them.

The apostles reported this to the church, and "when they heard that, they lifted up their voice to God with one accord, and said, Lord, thou art God, which hast made heaven, and earth, and the sea, and all that in them is" (Acts 4:24). Then they went on to quote Psalm 2, thanking God for His protection of their leaders. These Christians used God's own words to thank Him. Do we have a better way to show appreciation for all God has done for us?

GUIDELINES TO PRAYING SCRIPTURE

How do you pray the scriptures? First, it's a good idea to ask God for help (Romans 8:26–27). The

Holy Spirit can give inspiration, and His wisdom can help us understand the scriptures and apply them to our lives.

We can use the psalms as examples of praise and worship. They are a great starting place when we don't know what to say to God. As we read the psalmists' appreciation for God's works, we recognize that He has done much in our lives too—and we can praise and thank God for His goodness. Pray God's truths back to Him to show appreciation for all He has done in your life.

Be certain your "prayer verse" relates to all Christians, and not just one situation. Sometimes in scripture God gave promises to a particular person or group; trying to apply them to your own life may lead to misunderstanding. For example, God's promise to Abraham to found a nation through him does not apply to anyone else, though it certainly blessed all people. However, many verses are meant for all believers, and these will bless your life if you pray them.

Use God's Word to direct your prayers. If you were about to ask God for something the Word prohibits, don't pray for it. And remember the balance of the Lord's Prayer—ask God to provide for physical needs, but don't pray greedily. Make certain you spend time in praise and thanksgiving as well as your own requests.

As we pray, let us also be aware of ways in which we ourselves can be the answer. If others need help that we can offer, God may direct us to give our own time or resources. As we pray about a leadership shortage in the church, could we fill that need? Or if someone in our circle of family or friends has a physical need, perhaps we ourselves can step up to meet the need.

EXAMPLES OF PRAYING THE SCRIPTURES

Here are examples of a few verses and how you could use them in your prayer time.

Praise: "I will sing to the LORD, because He has dealt bountifully with me" (Psalm 13:6 NKJV). Perhaps you could combine this verse with a praise song telling of God's wonderful love. Psalms is the songbook of the Bible, so singing in connection with them is appropriate. Then meditate on the many ways God has dealt bountifully with you, praising and thanking Him for those blessings. Praying the psalms can become very personal when you connect their truths to your own life.

Additional praise psalms to use in your prayer time: Psalm 28:6–7, 59:17, 100:1, 101:1, 103:1–5. Many other psalms can be used as prayer and praise starters; it will not take long for you to find something you can relate to.

Confession: "If we confess our sins, he is faithful and just to forgive us our sins, and to cleanse us from all unrighteousness" (1 John 1:9). Thank God that He is willing to forgive your sins, and consider the sins you may have in your life. Is there some sin that simply slipped under the wire while you were not looking? Or something you haven't wanted to face, because you fear giving it up? Confess any failure you're aware of, and then ask God to convict you of any unintentional, unknown sins—and to show you how to remove them from your life. Agree with God that these sins will no longer have a hold on your life, and ask His help to avoid them in the future.

Additional verses for confession: Psalm 32:1–4, 51:1–4; Proverbs 28:13; James 5:16.

Thanks: "I love the LORD, because He has heard my voice and my supplications" (Psalm 116:1 NKJV). Think about the many times God has heard your prayers and answered them—and be thankful. If you are in a dry spell, when prayers do not seem to be receiving answers, talk to the Lord about that. Is there a sin that is blocking the way?

Are you determined to have something that God does not want you to have? Are you simply being impatient?

Even if you have not noticed prayers answered recently, recognize that there are still things you can thank God for. For hundreds of years after the event, the Israelites remembered that God had rescued them from Egypt, and they praised Him for that. Has God favored you in the past with blessings that still impact you today? Thank Him for them.

Additional verses for thanks: 1 Chronicles 16:8–12; Psalm 30:4, 75:1, 92:1, 106:1, 119:62; 1 Corinthians 15:57; Philippians 4:6; 1 Thessalonians 5:18.

Supplication: "Be anxious for nothing, but in everything by prayer and supplication, with thanksgiving, let your requests be made known to God" (Philippians 4:6 NKJV). Recognize that God is more than willing to answer prayer—even your smallest ones. You do not have to be a spiritual giant to see God respond to your praying. He invites the humblest Christian to pray, and He is willing to answer. Never let fears overtake your requests, but honestly go to God and ask. Then leave the response to Him.

Additional verses about supplication: Psalm 6:9, 31:22; Matthew 7:7–8; John 14:13–14; Ephesians 6:18.

Connecting the scriptures to your requests will keep your prayers on course and bring great blessing into your life. God wants a close connection with you, and combining your prayers with His Word will help bring that to pass.

8. When Prayer Is Hard

Some days prayers burst easily from our lips. We feel so close to God that it's only natural to communicate with Him. We are communicating directly with God's heart, and the communion is sweet.

Shouldn't prayer always be that way? It's not.

There are also times when it seems as if prayer is wrenched from our hearts. Or we simply don't want to open ourselves up to God. Maybe we resent a situation we're in or fear that if we let God control our lives, He will make us do something we don't want to do.

When we feel that way, we need to take a step back and realize that something is wrong. Either we have fallen into sin or Satan is trying to divert us from the path that will be productive in God's kingdom. When our desire is to do the Lord's will, He will make a way for us, no matter what He calls us to do. Serving Him will become a pleasure rather than something we dread.

If we're struggling to pray, we don't have to stay in this situation. We can ask ourselves some questions that may help us understand and solve our prayer problems.

Could Sin Be Separating Me from God?

Most often, when we no longer feel like praying, some sin has come into our lives to separate us from the Lord. Guilt over choices that displease Him makes us uninterested in praying. Sometimes we're not even completely aware of the cause, but like a computer with a hidden virus, things just aren't right. As we fail to recognize what caused our separation, we struggle to pray.

Once we've identified the sin that's blocking our prayer life, we need to pray the most. And in turning to prayer, we're turning to God. As we honestly confess our sin and its effects, He can make our rough paths smooth. This may require some hard spiritual work, but it will be well worth it.

Afraid of confession? Remember that trying to hide from God is useless—He knows all our sin and doubt, and He is willing to help with them if we ask (1 John 1:9). The righteousness we gain from confession is a precious spiritual treasure.

Is sin hard to give up, or does the temptation seem too strong? Tell God about that too, asking Him to help you get beyond them. It may help to break your confession into smaller pieces, dealing with aspects of the sin one at a time. Begin by telling God that you know something in your life is wrong, and you want to give it up—but you need His help. Honestly ask God to work in the hard parts of your heart—those parts that you can't even begin to change on your own. As you bring these burdens to God, He can give you a breakthrough. God will show you the bigger picture, cause you to hate the sin as He does, and help you turn from wrongdoing through the power of the Holy Spirit.

AM I SEEKING GOD WHOLEHEARTEDLY?

God makes it clear that He is not looking for half-hearted believers. Wavering followers are fairly useless to His cause and provide no positive witness of His works. Instead, God calls us to rely on Him, to go to Him when we need wisdom, and to trust in Him:

> *If any of you lack wisdom, let him ask of God, that giveth to all men liberally, and upbraideth not; and it shall be given him. But let him ask in faith, nothing wavering. For he that wavereth is like a wave of the sea driven with the wind and tossed. For let not that man think that he shall receive any thing of the Lord. A double minded man is unstable in all his ways.*
>
> JAMES 1:5–8

Humans often find it easier to doubt than trust. We may have agendas of our own, and we'd like God to rubber stamp them. Or perhaps we'd like Him to give us one thing when He has other plans. Even the good things that God intends to do in our lives can separate us from Him if our hearts aren't fully aligned with His will. We want, but we don't want God's will. When that is our mind-set, we will receive very little and probably feel far from the Lord.

But that does not mean God wants to leave us in that confusing place. Instead, His Word says, "draw nigh to God, and he will draw nigh to you. Cleanse your hands, ye sinners; and purify your hearts, ye double minded" (James 4:8).

Moses recorded a similar promise God made to the ancient Jews, that even serious spiritual failure could not fully separate them from God if they were willing to turn back to Him. "But from there you will search again for the LORD your God. And if you search for him with all your heart and soul, you will find him" (Deuteronomy 4:29 NLT).

Closeness to God may seem elusive when we have doubts. But if we do not give up, if we are willing to become wholehearted believers, we have not come to the end of our road. We must accept that God knows more than we do (He knows *everything*, actually), and seek His will.

Then we can step out in trust, knowing that He will do what is right and good, even if our way is hard. In the end, we will find that any hard work we put into our spiritual lives was worthwhile.

AM I IN A DRY TIME?

Having a dry period doesn't mean you're a spiritual failure. Even the biblical prophets had spiritually arid times, but they didn't allow themselves to stay in them.

Dry times may be a result of sin in our lives, as noted earlier. Or we may have done nothing wrong and are just facing a time of testing that will lead to growth. (Consider Job and his trials.) If God always seemed close, how little faith would be required of us. But when He seems distant, we are forced to trust. We can build our faith that He is still working on our behalf, even when life seems dark. In times of dryness, God is building our spiritual muscles. Though it may not feel pleasant, it will bring us great benefit in the end.

When we need joy, we can trust God to provide it. When Ezra read scripture to the formerly exiled Jews—people who had returned to their homeland after being in bondage for so many years—they were upset over things they had not known and the ways in which they had unknowingly disobeyed God. But Nehemiah encouraged them to celebrate and rejoice in God, "for the joy of the LORD is your strength" (Nehemiah 8:10). God did not want to punish them; He wanted them to know how they should live for Him. And joy is part of the Christian life.

AM I WORRYING?

Worry is a real prayer killer because it attempts to put us, instead of God, in charge of every detail of our lives. Though Jesus told us not to worry and explained its utter uselessness (Matthew 6:25–27), we often pull difficult situations back into our laps. It's as if not worrying might make things turn out badly. . .or God could not handle these things for us. These are lies of Satan that keep us wound up in ourselves instead of trusting God.

Worry epitomizes a lack of trust in God—even a pride that says *we* might be able to do better than God, if He would just let us. Many of us get caught up in agonizing about our past, present, and future, even being concerned about things that are unimportant or may never happen to us. But 1 Peter 5:7 tells us to cast all our cares (or anxieties) on God, who cares for us. The only way to do that is pray, and when the problem does not seem to go away, we can "pray without ceasing" (1 Thessalonians 5:17).

God will never drop the ball, and if we worry that He will, we clearly do not understand His power or His love for us. As we recognize that God is in control, and nothing we can do apart from Him will improve any situation, we pray and live in faith.

AM I SIMPLY NOT PRAYING?

Sometimes prayerlessness comes from busyness. We may get out of the prayer habit because the things of this world have dragged us in another direction; then, when we do try to meet with God, communication seems all the more difficult. Neither we nor God are happy about the break in our relationship.

If life is busy, it's a good idea to fit in prayer wherever you can. Though having a specific time and place for prayer is best, it's still possible to fit prayer into the "gaps" of the day—as you sit in a doctor's office or on the drive to work or when you're waiting for your child after baseball practice. Even brief times of prayer and praise can feed your soul temporarily—but get back to a regular schedule as soon as possible.

The good thing about busy prayers? Perhaps, when life calms down again, you can continue the habit of praying wherever you are so that your prayer is truly ceaseless. God never wanted only occasional communication.

Do I Let Other Things Distract Me?

This is an old method of Satan's to keep us from one of the most powerful things we can do in our spiritual lives. People who mean to pray, but suddenly have several "important" things crop up, need to recognize that the enemy will always have some distraction for us. The devil can make many things seem more important (or more pleasing) than spending regular time with God. Putting God first and spending time with Him may even make some "emergencies" suddenly disappear.

It's easy to get distracted *from* prayer, and just as easy to be distracted *in* prayer. You plan to spend time with God, but unless you keep your mind focused on prayer, it's easy to start thinking about all the things you have to accomplish today, rather than praying wholeheartedly. But there are solutions to these distractions. First, when a something else comes to mind, pray about it. It may soon lose its mental grip. If need be, keep a pad and pen nearby and write down the distraction, so you can deal with it after you're done praying. But continue in prayer until your communion with God is complete.

It's also helpful to keep a prayer list. This helps to reduce distractions, and it keeps you from suddenly not knowing what to pray for. This list can also capture praise items as you see God answer your prayers.

A final thought: sometimes we carry such a burden in our lives that we seem unable to pray for anything else. As soon as we begin to pray, we slip right past praise, confession, and thanksgiving into our own needs. God understands these times in our lives, but always remember that praise can lighten your heart. Even if we do not begin in praise, it needs to be part of our prayer experience.

AM I REMEMBERING TO PRAISE GOD?

The importance of praising God can hardly be overstated. Lack of praise makes prayer dull, because when we fail to appreciate who God is and what He has done, we're focusing on ourselves. But it's the Lord who is our solution to every problem!

Like the biblical Israelites, who often remembered how God had led them safely out of Egypt and into the Promised Land, we can offer repeated thanks for the milestones in our lives—the important works of God. Even His work in our less-than-spectacular daily lives can make for appropriate praise. Did He get you safely to work today? Did He provide for your basic necessities? Did He give you the love of family or friends? There is never a time when praising God is not appropriate (Psalm 34:1).

Have we spent time in awe of God's love and power? If not, our prayer lives are out of balance, and we should get them back in line with thanksgiving. If you don't know where to start, choose a psalm and ask yourself what it tells you about God. How you can praise Him for that? How does that praiseworthy attribute of God relate to your life today?

AM I TRUSTING AND HOPING IN GOD?

We all have days when trouble assails us—some of us have weeks, months, or even years of trial. But hasn't God helped us before? And, based on that, can't we trust Him to do so again? When we focus on the negative and begin to worry, our faith slips. But God is still powerful and will lift us up if we trust and hope in Him (Proverbs 3:5–6).

The challenge of trust is to remain faithful under trial. It may be hard to do that, but we have God's promise: "That the trial of your faith, being much more precious than of gold that perisheth, though it be tried with fire, might be found unto praise and honour and glory at the appearing of Jesus Christ" (1 Peter 1:7). Whatever we suffer, however little we understand, we can be sure that these trials have a purpose. One day they will honor Jesus, when He appears again.

Are you feeling discouraged from trial after trial? Trust that God is making a chain of glory that will honor Him. And share those emotions with Him, knowing that He cares about them, loves you, and wants to support you. Trust in God will be richly rewarded.

AM I DELIGHTING IN GOD?

Knowing Jesus is not an empty or constantly painful experience. If that were so, it would not be much of a relationship, would it? God wants us to delight in Him (Psalm 37:4), just as He delights in us, His sons and daughters (Zephaniah 3:17). These verses describe a deep, intimate relationship on both sides, one that is embodied by trust and caring.

For various reasons, we may be tempted to believe that God is not loving. If we think of the Lord as a mean, judgmental God who only pours out wrath, we have been deceived by Satan. Even the darkest parts of scripture have a hint of God's love in them.

Jesus provided a beautiful picture of how those who repent of their sins will always be welcomed into the Father's arms—it is called the parable of the prodigal son (Luke 15:11–31). One son left his father, taking all his inheritance, and wasted everything in a far land. The father, knowing things would not end well, was ever on the lookout for the young man, until he finally returned— embarrassed and empty-handed. But despite the boy's sin, the father received him with joy. The picture applies to us too, because God's love never ends.

Do we delight in God because we know His loving nature and trust in that love? It will make all the difference in the world to our prayers.

AM I A PRAYER WARRIOR?

There's a reason for the phrase "prayer warriors"— prayer takes spiritual strength and commitment, much like what a warrior carries into battle. Do not be fooled: we have an enemy who can only be overcome through prayer. Satan, who began opposing mankind in the garden of Eden, has not given up on his goal of turning people away from God.

If we had to enter this battle alone, "our striving would be losing," as Martin Luther wrote in the hymn "A Mighty Fortress." The enemy is stronger than we are, but the battle remains under God's control.

Always remember that prayer is part of the battle. As you pray for an unsaved friend or family member, for example, you are engaging in spiritual warfare—and the enemy will not give up easily. Keep fighting, using the weapon God has given you. Prayer is most powerful on the offensive.

DON'T GIVE UP!

Have you ever prayed for something for a long time, and suddenly God answered your prayer? Did you then think that long period of prayer had been a waste? Probably not. Be consistent in prayer, and God may surprise you with an answer that is even better than you expected.

Difficult prayer does not equal unsuccessful prayer. A very hard field might be difficult to plow, but could also yield a bountiful crop. Challenges in prayer may eventually lead to great spiritual victories.

9. Other Tips for Praying

We've covered a lot of ground to this point— a summary of prayer from each book in the Bible, 144 verses relating to prayer, the Lord's Prayer, Jesus' example of prayer, praying the scriptures, and difficulties in prayer. Now here are a few final tips on what to expect in prayer, how to pray, and what to pray for.

We can become aware of some things that will enrich our prayer lives. We should:

1. put our lives in order every day. We can confess our own weakness and disobedience, asking God to put these things in line with His will. If we combine Bible study and prayer, God can use scripture to convict us of the things we need to change in our lives. As we prayerfully focus on these needs, He will help us.

2. become aware of the awesome things God has done for us or is willing to do through us. Praise is the appropriate response to the good things God has already done in our lives.

3. become aware of needs in the lives of others that we can help fill. Do we need

to give money, time, or effort to reach others for Christ? Every day we can pray about the ways God wants us to reach out for Him.

4. look forward to a day lived for God. As we face a busy schedule, we could easily be distracted from the things God has in mind for us to do. Asking His help with priorities and keeping on track can head us in the right direction.

Here are a few more thoughts that may help us develop an intimate prayer relationship with the Lord.

PRAYER WILL NOT ALWAYS EXCITE YOU

Don't expect your quiet time with God to be incredibly exciting every day. Married people know that there are special times together, but many days are fairly ordinary. That does not mean the husband and wife don't love each other. In the same way, not every meeting with God will be unusually special. But just as spouses daily continue to do ordinary tasks like laundry or mowing the lawn, you'll need to continue to pray even when prayer lacks adventure.

We cannot live in constant excitement, but

we can live in steady love. Know that even on days when you are not topping the mountains in prayer, a time is coming when you will be thrilled by what God does in your life. Often these special days come after some of your greatest trials.

PRAISE GOD FERVENTLY AND REVERENTLY

Unwilling praise makes for wimpy prayers. If you do not feel like praising God, you'll need to address the reasons behind that feeling. Are you disappointed because God has not given you something you desired? Do you feel bitter toward Him? Perhaps He has something better in mind for you. Remember, God foresees your future and rules your whole life. Trust that He will put you on the best path, not just a good one, if you rely on Him.

When we can accept God's will for our lives, we are freer to praise Him. Believe in the praise you offer to God—He is not looking for a false worship forced past our lips. Reverent prayer recognizes the greatness of our Lord and does not take Him for granted or think of Him as someone who should be at our beck and call. It can see the advantage of a powerful Lord who is worthy of our worship and wants to be part of our lives.

Pray Intimately

Remember that God has made you and loves you. If you have accepted Jesus as Savior, you are His friend. Talk to Him about all the things on your mind. Does something worry you? Is there a goal you'd like to reach? Are you concerned for a friend or family member who is going down a wrong path? You can share these concerns, and everything else, with Jesus.

Pray Honestly

Do not tell God what you think He wants to hear. Don't worry about praying "correct" prayers, or some prayer that another person has prescribed for you. This relationship is between you and God— and He will guide you in the best way to relate with Him. Whatever you need, whatever concerns you, pour it out to Him. If you feel angry or fearful or discouraged, explain those feelings to God. He can handle it, and He'll help you get beyond the emotion to true faith.

Ask in Faith

Ask with the expectation that God *will* supply your needs and the needs of others (Matthew 21:22; Mark 11:24). It is easy to pray without really believing that God will take an interest and respond, but such prayers do not get much response from the Lord. If you have doubts that God will really answer, discuss that with Him in prayer. Intentionally stretch your faith by believing that God will give a wonderful answer, and you may see that happen. But know that spiritless, doubtful prayers don't do much for anyone.

Have you asked in faith, truly seeking the Lord's will in some matter? Then take 1 John 5:14 as your promise: "This is the confidence that we have in him, that, if we ask any thing according to his will, he heareth us." If you have prayed for something that is good and, as far as you know, in God's will for your life or another's, trust that He will hear and respond.

WHOM SHOULD I PRAY FOR?

Do not be selfish in prayer, thinking only of yourself. Be aware of your world—pray for those who are persecuted for their faith, for your enemies, and those who do not know the Lord.

Pray for God's will to be done and for Him to work in others' lives. You may pray for anyone with a need, even if you have only seen or heard of their need. Pray for your church and church leaders and ministries and other Christians (Ephesians 6:18). Pray for your government, both locally and nationally (1 Timothy 2:1–2).

However, while you don't want to become overinvolved in praying for your own needs, don't forget to pray for yourself. Recognize your own failures and needs, asking forgiveness and help for your physical and spiritual limitations. God is interested in hearing everything about you, because He loves you and wants to help.

BE VOCAL IN PRAYER

If a problem is overwhelming, perhaps you need to get away with God in private and have an out-loud conversation with Him. It was not uncommon for Jews of the Old Testament to pray aloud; remember Daniel, who publicly prayed when it was most dangerous (Daniel 6)? Actually voicing your problems to God can be helpful in sorting them out.

PRAY WITH OTHERS

Prayer doesn't have to be done alone. You can join a prayer group and find great support. If your church has a prayer chain, sign up to receive requests and pray for them regularly. Not only will this be good for your prayer life, it will help you build a sense of community with others in your congregation.

ALWAYS RELY ON GOD

Finally, if you have doubts about your prayer life, you can always bring them to God. He is the Master of communication with frail humans, and He does not expect more of us than we are capable of. Just as the disciples asked Jesus to teach them to pray, we can too. As we trust in Him, He will show us the way to better interaction with Him.

Use these tips to build a strong relationship with the Lord. . .and a powerful prayer life. God desires this kind of relationship with His people—including you!

10. NOW PRAY!

Perhaps the most important key to prayer is to make it a regular habit. Otherwise, time slips by and our most important relationship is set aside for other, less important things. God will not bang on your door to remind you to pray—but other things will certainly push themselves into your life as distractions.

Remember, it's your choice: to let other things drag you away from God or to keep a regular commitment to spend time with Him. It can be a challenge, but it is never impossible. And if you wander away from a regular quiet time, God will always welcome you back.

But better than returning to God is simply keeping your commitment to communicate with Him. When that seems difficult, here are some final thoughts that may help.

MAKE A COMMITMENT TO PRAYER

Set up a time each day to pray, and, if at all possible, read God's Word then too. Should you miss your scheduled time, pray as soon as you realize what's happened.

And when you have a few minutes, pray

wherever you are—on the bus or train to work, as you wait in line in the bank or grocery store, or when you see someone who has an obvious need. Pray for people you know, and for those you've never met. Make your family a regular part of your prayers. Lift up your church, your pastor, and other ministries. There is no lack of things to pray for when you attune yourself to God's will and the lives of those around you. If you find yourself praying repeatedly for the same things, ask God to open your eyes to new prayer needs. You may be amazed at how many things He'll show you.

Creating a regular prayer schedule may require sacrifice. Time in prayer means you cannot spend as much time with television or a favorite hobby. But think of God as a friend you shouldn't neglect. After all, isn't He the best friend you can have? Who else will repeatedly listen to every detail of your worst, worrying problem without a complaint? Who can provide real solutions to the problems you've agonized over?

EXPECT ANSWERS

When we faithfully bring problems to God, He may provide amazing solutions. Unexpected people can give us support—even folks we never knew or someone we'd done no more than say "hello" to in passing.

Perhaps you've been praying for a loved one in a terrible situation. Do not give up! God's best answer may be on the way, if you only remain faithful. The health situation you thought was chronic might be solved by a change of doctors or medication. The unsaved friend or relative can be convinced by the most surprising person or circumstance. Pray in trust that God *will* work in their lives.

Occasionally, you may be the answer to a problem. Don't hesitate to turn prayer needs into solutions by making your hands God's hands. Ask God, "Can I help?" and "Should I help?" If He prompts you to become involved, do it immediately.

COMMIT TO HONESTY

Prayer isn't just asking God for pleasurable things—or even for the good of other people. It is sharing with Him our whole lives, even the less wonderful parts, seeking His counsel and aid.

We must pray about our own failings and weaknesses. Prayers that only focus on our own strong points tend to make us proud, but when we humbly admit to God that we fail, He can bring spiritual growth into our lives.

Surely you know at least some flaws in your best friends' lives. That doesn't mean you don't love them anymore. In the same way, God loves you despite your less-than-perfect parts. But far more than your friends, He can help you overcome any weakness you are willing to share with Him. It may take time, but confession and praying for God's help work.

WHEN YOU DON'T KNOW WHAT TO PRAY

Perhaps a situation—yours or others'—seems too bleak for words. You look at it and just feel perplexed. What should you do?

God doesn't expect you to possess all knowledge. . .that's His job. You don't need to tell God the best solution to any problem; simply bring the need before Him. Ask God to work in His own wonderful way and bring hope to the situation. The solutions that come may not be what you expected, but you can trust that God has a plan that will outdo anything you could have suggested.

WHEN YOU FEEL WEAK

If you are feeling weak spiritually, "Seek the LORD and his strength, seek his face continually" (1 Chronicles 16:11). Paul learned this truth when he had a "thorn in the flesh" that God would not remove, even though the apostle prayed for that three times. God replied: "My grace is sufficient for thee: for my strength is made perfect in weakness" (2 Corinthians 12:9). Paul's response?

> *Most gladly therefore will I rather glory in my infirmities, that the power of Christ may rest upon me. Therefore I take pleasure in infirmities, in reproaches, in necessities, in persecutions, in distresses for Christ's sake: for when I am weak, then am I strong.*
>
> 2 CORINTHIANS 12:9–10

When we become keenly aware of our own lack of strength, there is still power in God's Spirit. If we feel confused or overburdened, we can count on the One who is never that way. Our very weakness gives God an opportunity to act within our lives, and it may become a testimony to His greatness.

Our greatest strength in prayer lies in the One with whom we communicate.

ANSWER THE INVITATION

God has issued a standing invitation to prayer. Take Him up on it. He is happy to lead you as you begin to communicate with Him. Don't worry about how you pray—there are many ways to do it. God is more interested in your heart than the specific form or words of your prayers.

While you pray, God may remind you of needs in your own life and the lives of others. Add these to your prayers, and you will find there is never a shortage of people and situations to pray over. Think of the ways God has worked in your life and the lives of others, and you will find there is never a shortage of praise to be offered. Prayer time can be a time of joy as you connect with the Lord, who has invited you to communicate with Him at an ever-deepening level.

So now, let us pray!